Making It
in
Book
Publishing

Leonard Mogel

Macmillan • USA

Macmillan General Reference
A Simon & Schuster Macmillan Company
1633 Broadway
New York, NY 10019-6785

An Arco Book

MACMILLAN is a registered trademark of Macmillan, Inc.
ARCO is a registered trademark of Prentice-Hall, Inc.

Library of Congress Cataloging-in-Publication Data
Mogel, Leonard.
    Making it in book publishing/Leonard Mogel.
        p.   cm.
    ISBN: 0-02-860593-4
    1. Publishers and publishing–Vocational guidance–United States.
I. Title.
    Z471.M7   1996
    070.5'73–dc20   95-34430
                                                 CIP

Manufactured in the United States of America

10 9 8 7 6 5 4 3 2 1

Book design by A. & D. Howell

To Michael Tolkin and Peter Pitts,
with respect and love

Contents

Part III ♦ The Wide Range of Trade Publishing Activity

Part IV ♦ How Books Are Sold

Part V ♦ Book Publishers' Resources

♦ Contents ♦

Part VI ♦ The Publishing Job Scene

Acknowledgments

◆

Appreciation goes to my wife, Ann Mogel, for her encouragement, and major contribution to this book. We did it again, for the sixth time. It gets easier, but no less fun.

My sincere thanks to my editor, Barbara Gilson, for her guidance and intelligent advice. Thanks, too, to production editor Chris Dreyer for a superb job.

I wish to thank the people who enhanced this book by agreeing to be interviewed: Betsy Nolan, Gina Wright, Stephani Hughes, Gene Brissie, Kristin Kliemann, and Richard Curtis.

My gratitude to Datus C. Smith for the use of his fine chart of the book publishing network.

To *Publishers Weekly* for its editorial excellence and as a source of valuable information in the writing of this book.

To Barbara Meredith of the Association of American Publishers for the use of some of their data on book publishing.

Part I

The Structure of Book Publishing

Chapter 1

◆

A Short History of Book Publishing

I n the ancient city of Alexandria, founded in 332 B.C. by Alexander the Great, the first best-seller appeared. Known as *The Book of the Dead,* it was inscribed on a papyrus roll in a simple, cursive writing style. An enterprising undertaker supplied copies to mourners who placed the "books" in tombs as the soul's passport to the afterlife.

During that period, Alexandria was an early center of learning and literary production in philosophy, literature, and science, as was Rome in the first century A.D. In Rome, original manuscripts were delivered by the authors to publisher-booksellers who then copied them on papyrus or parchment rolls. Papyrus is made from strips of the papyrus plant that are laid together, soaked, pressed, and dried. Parchment is the skin of sheep or goats.

Titus Pomponius was the first publisher of Rome, and the first celebrity author was Cicero, the famed statesman and orator.

In the Dark Ages, books were reproduced by their authors and, later in this era, by the great monastic orders. The introduction of paper, first produced in China in A.D.105, into Europe gave rise to a new class of bookmakers, the scriveners (who actually "scribed" books) and the *stationarii* (who served as resident booksellers).

By the twelfth century, paper mills were already set up in Europe. In the fifteenth century, with the invention of movable type by German printer Johann Gutenberg, the demand for paper and the printing of books proliferated.

It is said that tens of thousands of books, predominantly of a religious nature, were printed during the Renaissance. Gutenberg's first work—the first book printed from movable type—was, of course, a Latin Bible, published around 1456. Gutenberg's invention spread throughout Europe and to England. In England, in 1476, William Caxton established his press and printed the works of Geoffrey Chaucer and others.

During the Reformation, in the sixteenth century, the English Crown banned the importation and circulation of heretical books. In fact, this ban made it necessary for a "pirate" publisher, John Danter, to be the first to publish Shakespeare's *Titus Andronicus*, in 1594.

The Pilgrims brought books to America in the early seventeenth century. Boston and Philadelphia were early centers of publishing. Benjamin Franklin published in the Quaker city, as did William Bradford, who, in 1693, became the first public printer in New York.

By the eighteenth century, great improvements had been made, particularly in the areas of paper, type, and presswork. France and England were early leaders in publishing, but Germany and Italy were not far behind.

One of the most dramatic factors in book production was the invention in 1884 of the Linotype machine by a German American, Ottmar Mergenthaler. If you have ever been in an old print shop and seen the printer hand-setting type character by character, you will realize how innovative the Linotype was, with an operator at a keyboard rapidly setting "lines" of type. Now, in the computer era, this method of typesetting seems as primitive to us as the clay tablets were to Gutenberg.

Book publishing and book selling flourished in America during the nineteenth century. In 1802, a "literary fair" was held in New York with twenty-four booksellers participating. Later that year, the New York Association of Booksellers was formed to publish and sell textbooks. Its first book was *Cicero* in Latin and English.

Most of the books sold in America during the nineteenth century were textbooks and imported books of English literature, of which Scott, Byron, and Wordsworth were favorites. After the Civil War, book prices came down, and many publishers and booksellers were established, principally in Boston, New York, and Philadelphia.

Founded in 1854, Ticknor and Fields published the work of many outstanding American authors of that era. It is still actively publishing today, as are a number of other publishers that originated then, including John Wiley & Sons, G. P. Putnam's Sons, and Harper & Brothers (now HarperCollins).

The American Booksellers Association (ABA) was organized in New York in 1900. This group still dominates the book business, sponsoring the annual ABA convention each June in Chicago.

The Book-of-the-Month Club, the first book club, was started in 1926, with forty-five hundred subscribers. By 1928, there were eighty-five thousand subscribers. Book clubs account for more than 4 percent of the multibillion-dollar gross annual sales of all books.

Paperbacks first appeared in America in the late nineteenth century, but didn't become popular until the late 1930s. The big growth in popularity of mass-market paperbacks occurred during World War II, when the industry discovered that soldiers were able to carry them around in their back pockets. Because the books were so cheap (ten cents in the 1940s), the GIs could read them, then dispose of them or pass them along to their buddies. Today, they cost $5.95 and up and are a major factor in book publishing, representing more than 16 percent of all book sales.

Chapter 2

♦

Book Publishing Today

These days, John Grisham tries to live a normal life as one of Oxford, Mississippi's, 10,141 citizens, although he may be its most prominent one, earning far more money from one book than another local literary hero, William Faulkner, made in a lifetime.

In 1989, Grisham was a thirty-four-year-old practicing lawyer when his first novel, *A Time to Kill,* was published. The book was hardly a blockbuster, selling only about five thousand copies. But in 1991 Grisham struck the mother lode with Doubleday's publication of *The Firm,* a novel about the nefarious deals of a Mafia-controlled law partnership. *The Firm* sold more than a half-million books in hardcover, and when it reappeared in paperback the next year, it sold better than *seven million copies.* Paramount Pictures' movie of *The Firm,* starring Tom Cruise, grossed more than $300 million worldwide. The lawyer-author's subsequent novels have had similar success, generating enormous advances even before he sits down at his word processor.

But don't assume for a nanosecond that Grisham's good fortune mirrors that of the whole book publishing industry. Each year publishers issue about three thousand new works of fiction. Few achieve success. Yet publishing is more than best-selling novels that become high-grossing movies. The industry, for example, publishes almost six thousand new books each year on sociology and economics, five thousand children's books, three thousand on medicine, two thousand on scientific topics, and two thousand on technology. In total, the twenty-six thousand publishers listed in the Bowker data file, an industry directory, produce almost fifty thousand new books every year. Of particular interest to readers, the burgeoning book business employs approximately seventy-four thousand people. And book sales in 1995 are estimated at $20 billion.

If you're seeking employment in this fascinating industry, you should know that not all publishers are giant organizations publishing a few hundred new books a year. Eleven thousand of the nation's publishers publish three or more books a year, while fifteen thousand publish fewer than three books each. For example, Minneapolis-based Better Endings New Beginnings published only one book in 1994 and has two books in print. Dinosaur Press in Tulsa published only two titles in 1994, its first year in business.

Where the Book Publishers Are

The *Literary Market Place* directory (*LMP*), available in most large libraries, lists almost seven hundred book publishers based in New York. Clearly The Big Apple dominates the publishing scene. Yet there is substantial book publishing activity all over the country. University presses, for example, exist at many major colleges and universities.

Massachusetts has about 150 publishers, including the major houses Little, Brown & Company and Houghton Mifflin. Illinois is home to a similar number of publishers, including Encyclopedia Britannica. There are about four hundred publishers in California, including many fine small presses and specialty publishers, such as Sierra Club Books and Sunset Books.

If you're going to work in book publishing, your options do extend beyond New York. One important consideration is money: You earn less in other cities. Of course, that may be balanced by the lower cost of living.

Chapter 3

◆

The Categories of Books

To gain an understanding of the categories of books, it is necessary to know that books are divided into various subsegments. We offer a basic description of each:

Adult trade books. Trade books are those created predominantly for the consumer and sold primarily through bookstores. They are also purchased by libraries for rental and reference. Among the categories of adult trade books are: cookbooks, health and recovery, mystery and suspense, romance, science fiction and fantasy, travel, biography, public affairs, gardening, poetry, sports, popular medicine, and the largest category, popular and classic fiction.

Religious books such as bibles, prayer books, devotional literature—fiction and nonfiction—also fit under the trade book umbrella. Many of these come from publishers whose output is exclusively religious books. In addition, some large general publishers such as HarperCollins have a religious book division. Others like Macmillan, Knopf, and Ballantine publish religious books as part of their regular lists.

Religious books are sold at conventional bookstores, religious bookstores, and at houses of worship. Bibles and other religious books are sometimes sold door-to-door. There are about thirty-five hundred religious bookstores in the United States.

Children's books (sometimes referred to as "juveniles"). Children's books include story and picture books for various age levels. These books are produced by trade book publishers and sold to retailers and to public and school libraries.

University press books. University press books are the products of the publishing offices attached to universities and colleges. They are issued largely to serve the specialized needs of the academic world and to college, university, and reference libraries. Many university presses also publish scholarly journals and textbooks.

Mass-market paperback books. Mass-market paperbacks are most often reprints of fiction and nonfiction books originally published as hardbound trade books. However, some are published only in the paperback format. They are softbound, smaller in size, printed on less expensive paper, and sell for a lower price than hardbound trade books.

Mail-order publications. These books are produced expressly for a consumer audience that purchases them as a result of a direct-mail or direct marketing solicitation. They are usually nonfiction books offering self-help and self-education on different subjects. Many of these books are sold as part of a series.

Book club books. Trade book publishers often license their books to book clubs that produce special editions sold through subscription sales plans.

Professional books. The professional category encompasses books for individuals that serve as educational tools in their professions and trades. They include technical, scientific, medical, legal, business, and reference materials. The field also includes directories and many professional journals.

College textbooks and educational materials. This category comprises books produced especially for college-level instruction and supplementary study. They are also used in adult continuing education programs.

Elementary and high school textbooks and learning materials. This category is sometimes known as "elhi" and encompasses all the books, teaching manuals, workbooks, guides, computerized learning programs, audiovisuals, and teaching aids produced for schools. They are sold directly to schools and school systems.

Subscription reference books. The rather substantial market of encyclopedias, dictionaries, atlases, and other reference works make up the subscription reference category division of publishing. These books are produced by large staffs of editors at reference divisions of publishers or by companies who publish them exclusively. Subscription reference books are sold through the mail, door-to-door, and to bookstores.

Summing Up

The largest categories are trade books, hardbound and paperbound. About thirteen hundred publishers produce books in this area. Some are small, publishing fewer than a dozen titles each year; others are large companies that publish a few hundred titles a year and are often owned by large communications companies.

In the *Literary Market Place (LMP)* listings there are about 75 publishers of dictionaries and encyclopedias, 22 of maps and atlases, 225 of juvenile and young adult books, and 340 of college textbooks.

There are also publishers that specialize in books on religion, nature, art, humor, travel, politics, crafts, and such special interests as spiritual science, hiking and river guides, poetry, science fiction and fantasy, psychiatry, and psychology. There's at least one publisher that produces blank books. If you have a strong special interest, consult *LMP* when you go job hunting. Book publishing's diversity may help you get the right job.

Chapter 4

◆

How Book Publishing Is Structured

T o understand how book publishing works, the entire publishing network must be analyzed. First we will examine the interaction and activities of suppliers, related companies, and individuals.

Although book publishing directly employs about seventy-four thousand people, tens of thousands of others are employed in book-related fields, thus offering job opportunities beyond the publishing organizations themselves.

The book publisher is at the center of the accompanying chart. Every position leads to or emanates from that spot, ultimately extending to the users of books at the bottom. We'll start from the top and work our way around the circle.

Authors

If the publisher is the hub of the publishing wheel, the author is clearly its principal spoke. This holds true whether the author is a bankable commodity such as John Grisham or Jeffrey Archer, a mystery or

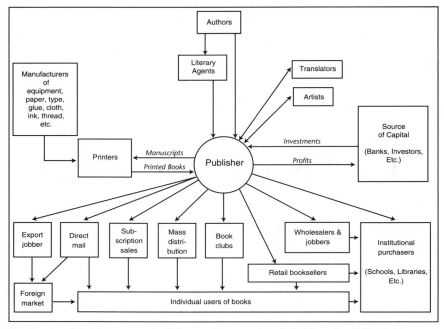

The book publishing network. (After a chart used in *A Guide to Book Publishing;* used with permission from the author, Datus C. Smith, Jr.)

science fiction writer, a "publish-or-perish" academic writing her first book, or a sports hero writing his memoirs with a ghostwriter.

Publishers advance megamoney to a small coterie of established authors, and expect these books to be best-sellers; otherwise they would not advance such staggering sums. The best-selling record to date, set in 1993 by Robert James Waller, is *The Bridges of Madison County,* which sold more than four million copies in one year.

What is the author's role in the acquisition process? To explain, let's trace the path from solicitation to publication. As a hypothetical example, let's use a well-crafted historical novel by an author with one published book.

First, the author writes an outline of the novel and fifty to one hundred pages and sends it to her agent. The agent reads the material, decides that it's commercial, and submits it to a few dozen trade publishers of hardbound fiction. The multiple submission assumes that the author's first publisher does not have an option that requires the next book to be submitted there first.

But even if the author's first publisher does not have this first refusal option, the agent will submit the material there in the first round, since it already has experience gained from publishing the author's work. We should also bear in mind that although this author has an agent, many authors do not.

Although the author of this historical novel is established, she must still present the outline and some sample writing as part of her submission.

After about three months of sending submissions to various publishers, the author's agent receives an offer from an editor at a medium-size publishing house. The editor offers $20,000 as an advance against future royalty earnings. The editor and agent negotiate, and finally a $25,000 advance is agreed upon. In the publisher's contract, not only are terms spelled out for hardcover publication of the book, but all subsidiary rights are specified as well. In this case, the author will share in subsidiary rights, receiving 50 percent of any income derived from the publisher's subsequent sublicensing of mass-market paperback rights, book club sales, magazine excerpts, foreign editions, and so on.

The $25,000 nonreturnable advance may seem to be a tidy sum if one has another full-time job, but if the author is to labor over this work for three or four years, the advance may seem insignificant.

The advance is paid in stages—usually a third on signing, a third at an agreed point during the writing process, and a third upon completion and acceptance of the manuscript.

Authors' advances vary greatly. We know that multimillion-dollar deals are made for such authors as Danielle Steel and Stephen King. But some authors don't receive any advance at all, even for long, scholarly works; others receive just $1,000 or $2,000.

If the average trade hardbound book sells six thousand or seven thousand copies, the author seldom receives more money than the advance. Such is the fate of our hypothetical historical novel. The book sells fifty-five hundred copies in hardbound, but never goes into paperback. For its author, her "profit" ends up as some good critical acclaim and a brief moment of glory. Then she is off to the library and the word processor for another three years to write another novel.

How a Publisher Handles Manuscripts

From a publisher's point of view, there are two categories of submissions: unsolicited and agented. With few exceptions, unsolicited manuscripts are not read and receive automatic rejection. Agented manuscripts are considered first for quality, and then on their conformity with the publisher's objectives.

Although a small number of publishers read every submitted outline and scan the sample chapter in their quest to discover new writing talent, most publishers regard this practice as too costly, hardly meriting the remote possibility of finding a masterpiece in the unsolicited muddle, or "slush," as it is typically termed.

When a submission passes the first level of acceptance, it then moves to a higher level of decision-makers, the managing and senior editors, with the final decision made by the editor-in-chief or publisher.

Before a publisher finally commits to publishing a book, other considerations come into play. Does the author seem to have the ability to deliver future works of similar quality? Is the author personable and articulate and capable of handling interviews, book signings, and publicity tours?

Once a book is accepted, the author works with an editor on fine-tuning the manuscript, stressing clarity, style, and organization. The whole procedure often takes years. Patience on the part of both the author and the editor is a necessity. In a succeeding chapter we discuss the editor's role in greater detail.

What Does a Literary Agent Do?

The 1995 *Literary Market Place (LMP)* lists about five hundred literary agents. They come in all sizes, from one-person operations working from home to large organizations with dozens of agents and entry to the sources of power at publishing houses and film studios.

The majority of manuscripts accepted by book publishers are submitted by literary agents. Since the agent represents other authors, he or she is familiar with many publishing houses. This puts the agent in the position of knowing where best to place a work.

A good literary agent reads the author's manuscript, makes suggestions on its presentation and content, submits it to a number of publishing houses, and ultimately negotiates the contract, which includes the advance and royalty rate paid by the publisher on behalf of the author.

Although hardcover royalties are somewhat standard—about 10 percent of the cover price of the book, with ascending rates based on the number of copies sold—an agent may be in the position to improve these terms, particularly in the area of increased royalties or bonuses if a book becomes a best-seller. Paperback royalties start at 6 or 7.5 percent. Almost all advances paid to an author are nonreturnable. If a book's sales do not reach the level advanced, the publisher takes the loss.

The agent also negotiates the author's share of subsidiary rights; that is, paperback, book club, broadcast and film, foreign, electronic, and serial rights. He or she also collects the author's royalties when they are due.

From the publisher's standpoint, the literary agent performs another function. The agent screens manuscripts before their submission, and presumably sends only the best proposals that fit the publisher's program, thus saving the publisher time and money. The literary agent can almost always reach the top acquisitions level at a publishing house. When a reliable agent calls the editor-in-chief at a major house and says, "I have discovered a brilliant new writing talent," the editor will almost always respond positively, since editors know that agents are placing their reputations on the line when making such a pitch.

How to Find a Literary Agent

Prominent literary agent Georges Borchardt has been in publishing almost fifty years. One of his earliest sales was Samuel Beckett's *Waiting for Godot* (to Grove Press for a $200 advance). Borchardt sums up the role of the literary agent:

We find, nurture, and produce the very things without which the industry could not function at all. Without agents, publishers would have to develop totally new departments within their firms, which would be very costly. It takes time to find the right writers, and to explain to writers what they can realistically expect— so that the relationship isn't always one of tension. Of course, we're always trying to get the best possible deal for the author, but we also act as a buffer.[1]

Reliability is always a consideration when dealing with an agent. Agents listed in *LMP* are among the most active in the field and must submit references to be included.

Many agents insist upon a fee before reading a manuscript. Others will not charge a fee but require a written description of the proposed book before a manuscript is submitted. One agent in New York, for example, charges $45 as a reading fee and asks for an outline and three sample chapters. The prestigious New York–based Janklow and Nesbit Associates does not charge a reading fee and requests only an outline and one sample chapter.

Another New York agent, Betsy Nolan, returns unsolicited manuscripts unread. She asks that authors first outline a project in writing; then, if she's interested in seeing more, submit the required elements. The Betsy Nolan Literary Agency does not charge for reading manuscripts.

Some agents specialize in fiction, others in nonfiction, and some both. Most of the larger literary agencies handle foreign markets, as well as film and TV rights.

The three largest Hollywood entertainment agencies are CAA, International Creative Management (ICM), and the William Morris Agency. They maintain substantial staffs of literary agents on both coasts.

Once an agent agrees to represent a writer, he or she will usually work on the entire presentation to make it as persuasive as possible to a publisher. An agent is more likely to become enthusiastic about an author if he or she thinks that there is a potential for additional works beyond the one submitted.

An agent and new client will usually sign an agreement establishing a commission rate, usually 10 percent (some agents receive 15 percent). The commission is payable on the author's advance, as well as on any additional royalties. It is also payable on all subsidiary rights transactions.

An agent may submit an author's manuscript to one publisher at a time or as a multiple submission. The agent may also conduct an auction when a property is sought by many publishers.

For an insight into the role of a literary agent, I talked to Betsy Nolan, a woman who has been active in this field for many years. Her comments:

Interview

After majoring in college in drama, philosophy, and English, I began work in the book business as a press agent. The years of rejection there made the pain of rejection as a literary agent a piece of cake.

My public relations background makes me look at a literary property in terms of how to sell it to the media. Since the whole thing is sales, sales, sales, this training proved very valuable.

As an agent, I have to sell the manuscript to the editor first. The editor then has to sell it to an editorial board, which has to sell it to the sales department, which has to sell it to the wholesalers and chains, which have to sell it to the bookstores.

The bookstores have to sell it to the retail customers, who, it is hoped, have been sold by seeing an ad or an interview set up by the marketing department of the publisher, which also has to have been sold on spending its budget for the book.

A new agent can expect to starve unless a Tom Clancy walks in and says, "I need you." Barring this, even when an agent does sell something to a publisher, there is a wait to get paid. There is some money on signing, some money on completion, some money on publication, and then forever between royalty payments.

Often, though, the only money an agent sees is the commission on the advance. The agent needs a lot of clients and some larger ones to make ends meet. Overhead needs to be kept at a minimum. I support my literary agency by doing public relations.

We agents sustain ourselves by thinking of Morton Janklow. This famous agent is reported to earn over $1 million a year from his literary clients—among them Sidney Sheldon, Judith Krantz, Jackie Collins, Shirley Conran, Danielle Steel, and William Safire. Clearly, 99 percent of all literary agents are not in his league.

Many East Coast agents now charge 15 percent instead of the 10 percent that exists in the entertainment business. When an agent negotiates a movie deal, the prices are usually high, and the commissions may vary.

Literary Agents of North America Marketplace, Fifth Edition, is an excellent reference book available from Research Associates International, Box 7263-L, FDR Station, New York, NY 10150-1910; the price is $33 plus $3.50 for shipping. The publication profiles a thousand agencies, including dramatic agents. A special introductory essay explains the do's and don't of dealing with agents.

We also recommend *Insider's Guide to Book Editors, Publishers, and Literary Agents! Who They Are! What They Want! and How to Win Them Over!*,[2] an excellent book for would-be authors that gives contact names at many publishers as well as a list of literary agents. Each listing gives background of agent, his/her recent titles sold, the best way for a writer to initiate contact, commission rate, reading fee policy, and approximate number of previously unpublished writers signed during the past year. The book also contains model book proposals and a sample query letter.

Translators

A gastroenterologist preparing a medical textbook on a particular phase of his specialty may require translation of articles in medical journals from a number of countries. The author and his publisher might consult the American Medical Writers Association for specialist writers in the languages required. They might then work with professional writers who understand medicine and are fluent in one or a number of foreign languages.

Or an author of an English-language version of a book might be asked to write two or three foreign-language editions. She and her publisher might then seek out a translator/writer who shares her sensibilities for the work and whose writing ability matches her own. This is often a difficult search.

LMP lists the names and capabilities of many translators. Some write in many languages. It takes expertise and proficiency to translate and to write professionally and in a specialized field. Columbia University has an agency that offers translating services in thirty foreign languages including such uncommon ones as Korean, Hindi, Serbo-Croatian, and Urdu.

Translators perform a unique function in book publishing. Their special talents make it possible for works of many important foreign authors to gain acceptance in the English language.

In one recent year, about fifteen hundred foreign-language books were translated into English for publication including about 400 from the German language, 370 from French, 170 from Russian, and 80 from Japanese.

The American publisher of the noted author Umberto Eco, who writes in Italian, will seek out an accomplished translator such as William Weaver to write the English-language version of Eco's work. At the Frankfurt Book Fair one can also see the large number of English-language books translated into other languages.

Translating, as with many other book publishing services, is often a freelance occupation, performed by home-based individuals. A fax, modem, and photocopier make it convenient for the translator to communicate with the author and/or the publisher.

The Wide Range of Editorial Services for Authors and Publishers

Although many of the services listed here are performed in-house at large publishers, it is often economically feasible for authors and publishers to employ freelance individuals and organizations to perform various functions in the publishing process. The current edition of *LMP* lists twenty-two separate categories of editorial services available to authors and publishers as follows:

Abstracting	Interviewing
Adaptations and Novelizations	Line Editing
Advertising and Promotion Copywriting	Manuscript Analysis
Bibliographies	Permissions
Broker for Manufacturing	Photo Research
Condensations	Illustration Agents
Copy editing	Proofreading
Fact Checking	Research
Ghostwriting	Rewriting
Indexing	Special Assignment Writing
Statistics	Translation Editing

There are even specialists who work on developing effective book proposals and improving manuscript ideas.

How does a publisher use these services? Let's say a publisher signs a contract with a movie superstar to write the story of her life. The actor is long on anecdotes and experiences, but short on writing and organizational ability. Either the star's publisher or agent recommends engaging the services of a competent "ghostwriter." (A ghostwriter is a person who writes a book for another person who is named or presumed to be the author.) The writer has frequent meetings and interviews with the author so that the writer will have the raw material to write the book. In addition, a researcher may be engaged to dig up additional background for the book. The ghostwriter may be paid a flat fee or enjoy a portion of the star's advance and royalty.

Another example of the use of freelance talent would be a large publisher's plan to produce a comprehensive illustrated history of Europe from 1900 through World War II. Rather than tie up its own editorial staff, the publisher might appoint a freelance editor, and then engage a team of consultants including photo researchers to track down appropriate photographs, writers, copy editors, proofreaders, book designers, artists, and other specialists.

Note the listing below for Carlisle Publishers Services as it appeared in the 1995 *LMP*. This company performs a comprehensive range of services, including "pre-press," which consists of all the elements of production until the book actually goes to press. Services such as these are used by publishers all the time to complement their own activities.

There are numerous services available to either write a complete book, ghostwrite, or polish a troubled manuscript.

> Carlisle Publishers Services
> Div of Carlisle Communications Ltd
> 4242 Chavenelle Dr.
> Dubuque, IA 52002
> TEL: (319) 557-1500   FAX: (319) 557-1376
> Mgr: Terrance Stanton
> Pres & Chmn of the Bd: John B. Carlisle
> CEO, Carlisle Commun: Sandra Hirstein
> Sales Mgr: Kim Hawley

> Full service project management & production group for publishers and others.

> Editorial services: copy editing, line editing, rewriting, typemarking, proofreading, permissions, photo research, indexing.

> Design & illustration services: book cover & interior design; calligraphy & lettering, layout, illustrations, computer graphics, mechanical drawings.

> Prepress services: photocomposition, desk top publishing, imaging, camera & completion services: computerized typesetting on XYVision systems, Linotron 202 & 300 word processing, telecommunications, electronic paging. All camera work, negative stripping & platemaking.

What a Book Producer or Packager Does

Book producers, as they prefer to be known, are individuals or companies who provide all the services necessary for a book's production, from concept to complete physical book, and delivery to a publisher's warehouse.

In the course of this service, book producers work with authors, agents, editors, designers, photographers, illustrators, typesetters, and printers. At times they go beyond these responsibilities and assist publishers in developing marketing plans for the books they produce.

How Book Publishing Is Financed

A book publishing enterprise may take many forms. It can be a large, publicly held corporation such as Harcourt General. It can be a small, privately held company, or it can be a limited partnership with backing from a number of investors.

For publishers, there is a slow payback. Authors' advances, manufacturing costs, and staff overhead must be paid before money comes back to the publisher from sales. Also, except for a runaway bestseller, a book publisher's profit comes from subsidiary sales; for example, paperback rights, book club rights, foreign rights, and so on. Thus, the publisher must wait for these revenues. In the interim, the company may require bank financing.

When a publisher enjoys a consistent period of profitable operations, it may be in a position to finance the business without loans, saving the costs of debt service. It may also choose to use excess capital to acquire other publishing and media enterprises.

Educational Purchasers:
Schools and Colleges

The school market represents elementary and high school textbooks, college textbooks, supplementary textbooks, audiovisual, and other materials. In total, it makes up better than $4.5 billion in annual sales, a substantial portion of all book sales.

This vast market presents unusual distribution difficulties. In the elhi field (elementary, junior, and senior high schools), textbooks are ordered at the state, city, and district levels, and, in some cases, by the individual schools.

At the college level, individual departments select their own primary and secondary textbooks. This selection is made after a review of all the available books in a particular discipline. The prescribed texts are then sold to students at the college bookstore, which is often owned by the college.

In colleges, supplemental texts are also adopted for use. Publishers employ skilled salespeople, once called "college travelers," who meet with professors and department heads in an effort to influence their decisions.

The adoption of a book by a teacher or professor doesn't mean that it cannot be replaced at a later date. Often a book written by a university professor will be adopted at his or her own school. Publishers, however, will not produce a textbook unless its potential sales extend beyond the limits of one or two institutions.

The Library Market

The library market represents a total sales figure of more than $1 billion per year. The group comprises about seventy-five thousand libraries in elementary, junior, and senior high schools, and about two thousand more at four-year colleges. In addition, there are approximately ten thousand public libraries.

Libraries may buy from publishers directly or, more often, through wholesalers or catalog operations, which simplifies the purchasing procedure. A library's discount from the publisher is less than that of a bookstore. Libraries generally buy hardbound editions, which are more lucrative to a publisher than paperback editions.

Publishers promote book sales to libraries by mailing catalogs and direct mail pieces. The sales staff or representative of a publisher will also visit large libraries directly and attempt to make sales of a large part of their lists.

Wholesalers and Jobbers

The operations of wholesalers and jobbers are vital to a publisher's distribution procedure. The terms are used interchangeably to describe organizations that stock books from publishers and ship them to bookstores and libraries. Some are huge businesses servicing the entire country. They function, in a sense, as clearinghouses by ordering fairly large quantities of each book on a publisher's spring and fall list. A small bookstore can then place orders with the jobber for one or two each of many different books from various publishers and have them all shipped the same day. For the bookstore, this method is much simpler than placing orders with each individual publisher. The bookstore pays the same price to the wholesaler that it would to the publisher, while the middleman, or jobber, receives a special discount from the publisher for ordering in large quantities.

Two of the largest wholesalers in this field are the Ingram Book Company and the Baker & Taylor Company. Baker & Taylor issues annual guides to elementary and secondary school libraries. In general, wholesalers and jobbers provide all types of books, from trade and technical volumes to school texts.

Wholesalers such as Ingram and Baker & Taylor service publishers' hardcover and trade paperback lines. Trade paperbacks are books that are larger and higher priced than mass-market paperbacks and are distributed primarily through bookstores.

Mass-market paperbacks are distributed through a network of about 550 independent wholesalers. These wholesalers, many of whom have a monopoly in a particular city, also distribute magazines and, in some cases, newspapers. Wholesalers also distribute mass-market paperbacks to air and rail terminals, newsstands, chain and convenience stores, supermarkets, and bookstores.

Retail Booksellers

Clearly, there are many different outlets that sell books. The predominant outlet for book sales, however, is the bookstore. There are about seventeen thousand bookstores in the United States, of which about ten thousand are general stores handling new books. Three book chains—Barnes & Noble (Barnes & Noble, B. Dalton, Bookstar, Doubleday, Scribner's), the Borders Group (Waldenbooks, Brentano's, Coles, Border's Book Shops), and Crown Books—dominate this market and account for one of every four books sold in this country.

Bookstores come in all sizes. About 70 percent of all bookstores are considered small business operations with a limited line of books. In contrast, the Barnes & Noble superstore on New York's upper West Side carries more than two hundred thousand titles. In the 1990s, the trend toward book "superstores" proliferated. A superstore is one with ten thousand or more square feet of space, and a stock of at least a hundred thousand titles. At the time of this writing, there are more than 400 superstores in operation, with many more in the planning stage.

Bookstores sometimes buy books directly from publishers, but more often from wholesalers and jobbers. The store's discount averages about 40 percent. In the past, bookstores could return all unsold books for credit. Economic need on the part of the publishers has limited this practice. In fact, some publishers do not now accept returns.

For guidance on what books to order, bookstores use a number of sources. Publishers' sales representatives who visit the stores may offer good information, as do publishers' catalogs. Attendance at the industry's annual American Booksellers Association (ABA) convention exposes the bookseller to the industry's total output of new books. Booksellers also rely on prepublication reviews from sources such as *Publishers Weekly, Booklist,* and *Kirkus Reviews.* In the postpublication period, booksellers consult the book review sections of *The New York Times Book Review*, the *Washington Post*, and other major newspapers and magazines.

C A R E E R   T I P

If you want to get a feel for books while you're still in college, getting a job at a chain bookstore is relatively easy, especially if you are willing to work odd hours. People who work in bookstores have been called "intellectual minimum wage slaves," yet the experience you get at the point of sale is beneficial in gaining a perspective on the entire book-marketing process and, ultimately, may lead to store management, book sales for a publisher, or sales representative. A sales rep is employed by a publishing company to sell its books in a given territory.

Book Clubs

There are 175 adult book clubs and 25 juvenile clubs listed in the most recent *LMP*. Book clubs account for more than 4 percent of publishers' net book sales.

The range of book clubs is truly eclectic. Some examples:

Astronomy Book Club	Aviators Guild
Catholic Book Club	Dance Book Club
Judaica Book Club	Mystery Guild
Performing Arts Book Club	Professional Chef Book Guild

There is a large club called the Get Rich Book Club, which claims 135,000 members and even publishes a monthly magazine.

Book club selections are marketed to the public and special groups directly by mail. Usually the publisher makes a book's printing plates available to the club, which then prints its own edition. Club members receive the books at a discount. The publisher receives approximately 10 percent of the club's price for each book printed. The author usually receives 50 percent of the publisher's net revenues from club sales. The prestige of being a club selection can significantly help a book's sales in bookstores.

Most book clubs are owned by book publishing conglomerates. Bertelsmann AG Publishers (which owns Doubleday, Dell, and Bantam) also owns the Literary Guild and many other clubs. Time Warner has owned the Book-of-the-Month Club since 1977. However, there seems to be no question regarding objectivity of clubs in their book selection process. Such selections are made on the basis of quality and commercial viability, not on whether the books come from the club's parent publisher.

The giant in the book club field is the Book-of-the-Month Club, known in the trade as BOMC. Launched in 1926, the club grew enormously in the post–World War II years. Recently its membership topped the three million mark. The average member is in his or her early 40s. Sixty percent of the members are women. Geographically, membership reflects the general population of the United States.

Each year, BOMC sends out about twenty-five million books. Unlike its chief competitor, the Literary Guild, which changes the books to fit its standardized format, BOMC reproduces the publisher's edition in the same size and format as the publisher.

An example of BOMC's clout in the book publishing business is its 1984 choice of the novel ...*And Ladies of the Club* by eighty-six-year-old Helen Hooven Santmyer as a main selection. As a result, the 1,176-page first novel zoomed onto the national best-seller charts. The club's choice in this case was no doubt based on the instincts of its editors and the unique quality of the book itself.

Mass Distribution

Mass-market distribution refers primarily to the mass-market paperback. Although the largest number of these books are reprints of fiction and nonfiction hardcover books, many are originals today, especially genre books in the horror, science fiction, romance, mystery, and western categories.

In the mass market, all books are sold on consignment (books shipped to a dealer that may be returned for full credit). This system results in a great deal of waste. Hundreds of new titles are published each month. The racks in most retail outlets can handle only fifteen or twenty titles and usually only the best-sellers prevail. Covers are stripped from the unsold copies and returned to the wholesalers. Compounding the problem is the lack of a market for these returns. Half of all books shipped to wholesalers remain unsold.

Yet mass-market paperbacks still maintain an impressive share of the entire book market, with annual sales well over $1 billion. The mass-market paperback publishers—Dell, Warner, Pocket Books, Penguin, and Bantam—have succeeded in this precarious field.

Subscription Sales and Direct Mail

We have all seen ads in magazines and received direct-mail solicitations for series such as Time-Life Books and Reader's Digest

Condensed Books. These "continuity" series and others in this category are big business in book publishing. They account for almost $700 million in their publishers' net sales.

Time-Life Books is the largest direct-mail book publisher, shipping twenty-five million volumes a year worldwide. Time-Life Books test-markets about twenty series ideas per year, but publishes only a small fraction of the total. Its best-selling series is *Home Repair and Improvement*, followed closely by *The Old West* and *Mysteries of the Unknown*.

Since their existence depends on huge sales, subscription and direct-mail books are carefully researched and designed so that they will enjoy wide consumer appeal.

Export Jobbers and Foreign Market

The Frankfurt Book Fair, conducted each fall, brings together hundreds of the world's book publishers for the purpose of selling foreign and translation rights to books. At Frankfurt, American publishers display their wares with the objective of selling rights to foreign publishers. They may also buy American or English-language rights to foreign books.

Similarly, each year at Bologna, Italy, a children's book fair is held. At a major American publishing house, there will be an individual or staff responsible for the sale of children's book rights; these people generally attend the Bologna fair.

To sell books in the foreign market, a publisher maintains an international sales force, or retains export jobbers. The export jobber has offices in key parts of the world, with a sales staff traveling to all the important book-buying countries. These salespeople call on bookstores, wholesalers, and libraries in their territories. The jobber is familiar with international trade customs and duties. Jobbers work for American publishers on a commission basis. While only about 5 percent of American adult trade hardbound and paperbacks are exported, from 10 to 20 percent of textbooks and professional books are sold in the foreign market.

Printers and Other Book Suppliers

Few, if any, publishers own their own printing plants. Large publishers often work on a contractual basis with their printers, thus guaranteeing firm prices and delivery schedules. In addition, American publishers use foreign printers as a source. Many art books, for example, are printed in Japan.

Publishers seldom purchase the individual elements needed for a book's manufacture, with the possible exception of paper. Large printers have their own binding facilities and are usually equipped with typesetting equipment. Other, smaller shops exist solely for the purpose of providing publishers and other customers with typesetting services.

We have now completed the full cycle illustrated on the chart, with all the supporting services of a book publisher's activities. In succeeding chapters we will take a closer look at other spokes in the publishing wheel.

Notes

1. Georges Borchardt, "Agent of Influence," *American Bookseller* (October 1989): 64.

2. Jeff Herman, *Insider's Guide to Book Editors, Publishers, and Literary Agents! Who They Are! What They Want! and How to Win Them Over!* (Rocklin, California: Prima Publishing, 1994-95).

Part II

Trade Book Publishing

Chapter 5

◆

An Overview of Book Publishing

I n the previous chapter, we discussed the book publishing cycle, describing the people and organizations who work with the publisher. Now, let's focus on the hub of this wheel, the book publishing organization and its people.

Clearly, there is a difference in the size of the staff of a small publisher such as Sierra Club Books, which publishes fewer than thirty books a year, and that of a giant like Simon & Schuster, which has revenues of $2 billion, employs about ten thousand people, and publishes hundreds of books a year through its various divisions. Yet the basic process of publishing a book is similar for both companies. The difference is the number of people performing each job category. At Sierra Club Books, there is one senior editor, while at Simon & Schuster's Trade Division, there are nine.

The following chart shows a typical table of organization of a trade book publisher. Not all publishers use the same titles. For example, the job of senior acquisitions editor in one company is titled project editor in another. In others, the title of executive editor does not exist. Also, the chain of command can vary from house to house.

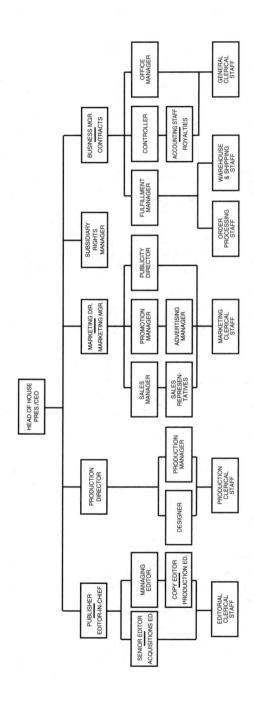

Few creative endeavors match the fascination of book publishing. Some time ago I met a man at a cocktail party who had been the president of a major book publishing house, had left that company for undisclosed reasons, and was "at liberty." I asked about his plans for the future. He replied, "I don't know where I'll go, but it will have to involve the written word." At the time, his response seemed pretentious, but on reflection I understand it.

There are about 220,000 jobs in book publishing, bookselling, and related fields. Is there one for you? Perhaps, but there are considerations. First, there's money. If you want to make $300,000 a year by the time you're thirty, get an M.B.A., a job in mergers and acquisitions, and read balance sheets instead of manuscripts. Book publishing is not a high-paying field, and entry-level salaries are low. On the other hand, upper-middle and top-level people in book publishing are paid as well as their counterparts in the media business. Salary increases tend to be in the range of 5 or 6 percent a year, comparable to other communications jobs.

In defense of low salaries, we must realize that book publishing is a low-profit business. The reasons are not simple. Although the price of books escalates each year, manufacturing costs have risen in the same proportion. Another factor is duplication of titles within a category. For verification, just look at the popular fiction, cookbooks, and self-help racks in your local bookstore.

Significant, too, are the high acquisition costs paid by publishers for works by proven authors. Not all those blockbuster, multimillion-dollar authors' advances result in multimillion-dollar profits for the publisher. The risks in this industry are profuse.

In book publishing, promotions to the top do not come as rapidly as they might in magazine publishing or advertising. A brilliant agency copywriter can become creative director and make more than $125,000 a year by the time he or she is thirty. Such a rapid rise is seldom achieved in book publishing. The pace in book publishing is more like a long-distance run than a sprint.

I read an article recently in a trade publication about the career track of a forty-one-year-old woman who was made publisher of a prestigious publishing house. She had, by the time of this appointment, spent fifteen years in publishing, starting with four years as an editorial assistant at two companies, and another eleven years as an acquisitions editor.

Another factor for consideration is job location. *Publishers Weekly (PW)*, the leading industry trade publication, reports that someone in book publishing will make six times as much money in New York, Chicago, or Boston than in Idaho.[1] Publishers in these cities offer much better pay than their colleagues in other parts of the country.

"It's largely a matter of scale," says *PW.* "The bigger the publisher, the higher the salaries; and big publishers tend to be located in major communications centers."

At publishing companies with annual revenues from $10 million to $50 million, the president or CEO earns the most money, followed by the heads of sales and marketing, production, editorial, subsidiary rights, art, and advertising and publicity.

In the giant publishing houses, those with annual revenues of over $50 million and up to $500 million or more, the salaries are indeed formidable. A president or CEO can make $750,000 a year, a sales vice president, $300,000, and an editor-in-chief, $175,000.

The book publishing industry is based heavily in New York. Almost 45 percent of publishing's book output comes from New York City and about one-half of its employees work there. Working in New York may be exciting and fulfilling, but is also expensive, especially on entry-level salaries. In the following chapter we define publishing jobs and note the salary ranges for each.

Notes

1. John F. Baker, "Your Personal Bottom Line," *Publishers Weekly* (April 25, 1994): 17.

Chapter 6

◆

Who Does What at a Book Publisher

The Association of American Publishers has divided publishing jobs into three basic areas: editorial, production, and marketing. Of course, not every company employs all the positions listed. Titles mean different things in different houses. We may, therefore, show three or four job classifications on the same line, basically applying to the same function. Later in this chapter, we define these jobs and note the salary ranges for each.

Editorial

Publisher/Editor-in-Chief/Editorial Director

Senior Editor/Acquisitions Editor/Project Editor/Textbook Editor/Procurement Editor

Managing Editor

Associate Editor

Copy Editor/Technical Copy Editor/Production Editor

Assistant Editor

Editorial Assistant

Production

Vice President Production/Production Director/Production Manager

Production Supervisor

Cost Estimator/Production Estimator

Art Director/Design Director

Designer

Production Assistant/Production Associate

Marketing

Vice President Marketing/Marketing Director

Market Research Manager

Sales Manager

Direct-Mail Manager

Promotion Manager

Sales Representative

Advertising Manager

Promotion Manager/Sales Promotion Manager/Promotion Specialist

Special Sales

Publicity Director/Publicity Manager

Subsidiary Rights Director/Subsidiary Rights Manager

Publicist

Copywriter

Marketing Assistant

Some of the job descriptions in this chapter have been taken from a report issued by the Association of American Publishers (AAP).[1]

Editorial Jobs

Publisher/Editor-in-Chief/Editorial Director: This top editorial position at a publishing house plans the editorial program, determines its staff needs, and hires and trains the senior editorial and supervisory staff. He or she also assigns responsibilities for implementing the editorial program, sets or approves program budgets and schedules, monitors and evaluates progress of the editorial program, and maintains liaison with the company's administrative, marketing, and production departments. Along with the senior and managing editors, he or she must have knowledge of market dynamics and be able to spot market trends. The salary range is from $80,000 to $136,000 for a publisher, and from $72,000 to $100,000 for an editor-in-chief or editorial director.

Note: The lower salary shown in this chapter for a particular job is for a publisher with revenues of less than $50 million annually. The higher salary is for publishers with revenues of $10 to $100 million or more. Bonuses and raises are not included. The average annual raise for employees in the *Publishers Weekly* survey is 6.9 percent.

Although practices vary from company to company and within job categories, the salary gap between men and women is often wider than the one between very large and small companies.

Senior Editor/Acquisitions Editor/Project Editor/Textbook Editor/Procurement Editor: The senior editor solicits and evaluates manuscripts and shepherds them through the publication process. He or she obtains management approval to acquire, contract for, and publish a manuscript (usually done in committee). He or she contracts with the author for a manuscript and, once a finished manuscript is submitted, edits it, working with the author to make any possible improvements in content, style, or organization. The editor also maintains the schedule and budget for the publishing project and supports the marketing effort. The salary range is from $51,000 to $93,000.

Interview

In an interview in Image World, *Gina Wright, developmental editor, nursing editorial, at the medical book publisher Mosby in St. Louis, discusses her role in the publishing process. (The role of development editor exists most often in textbook and technical publishing.)*

I formulate developmental plans to ensure products meet company standards and market needs. This involves meeting with authors, analyzing the competition and market needs, and identifying market trends. I commission artists and reviewers, manage project-specific budgets, and assess content for adherence to the development plan.

I see that manuscripts or multimedia products are processed and transmitted to production to ensure a timely publication. This involves working closely with the editing, production, design, and manufacturing departments.

In addition, I act as an information resource to ensure successful marketing of products. This involves creating summaries of new product information, reviewing advertising brochures and other copy for accuracy and clarity, and assisting in preparation and presentation of product and competitive information at sales meetings.

Managing Editor: The managing editor coordinates the progress of scheduling and production in fulfillment of an overall book and project program and works with marketing and production managers on planning. This person hires and trains staff for editing services, establishes editorial guidelines, oversees procedures for hiring freelance copy editors and proofreaders, assists in preparation of the editorial director's budget and publication schedule, and develops procedures for controlling flow from the manuscript to the finished product. The salary range is from $40,000 to $67,000.

Associate Editor: The associate editor screens and recommends manuscripts; handles rewriting and revision, often working with authors; and works with production, art, and other areas. He or she makes recommendations for authors and consultants, may function as project editor, and may undertake ad hoc assignments for the managing editor/editor-in-chief. The salary range is from $30,000 to $45,000.

Copy Editor: The copy editor handles assigned manuscripts by copyediting for style consistency, spelling, grammar, and punctuation. He or she also confers with editors on manuscript matters dealing with inconsistencies in style and information, and makes sure manuscripts comply with house style. The salary range is from $30,000 to $49,000. (The entire copyediting and proofreading functions are often "farmed out" by publishers to freelancers, who can make from $10 to $18 per hour [about $500 for the average manuscript], for copyediting and developmental editing.)

Assistant Editor: The assistant editor works with the associate editor, project editor, and authors on deadlines for submissions of material, assists the project editor in various areas such as consultant acquisition, and submits regular project reports to the project editor. The assistant editor must be able to function as project editor if necessary. In the textbook field, he or she is also responsible for implementing field-test designs, whereby manuscripts for textbooks are read by academics and focus groups for their comments before publication. The salary range is from $20,000 to $32,000.

Editorial Assistant: Since many of the readers of this book will be competing for the entry-level job of editorial assistant, we will discuss its functions in greater detail than the other jobs in this chapter. The often overworked and always underpaid editorial assistant is at any one time engaged in the following activities:

♦ Slush pile reader: In chapter 4 we defined "slush" as unsolicited manuscripts. At publishing houses that return these manuscripts unread, it is the editorial assistant's job to send them back with the appropriate statement of the company's policy.

If there is time, the editorial assistant may muddy his or her hands in the pool of slush. In the unlikely event that a promising manuscript turns up (less than 1 percent), it is given to an editor for evaluation.

♦ Manning the phones: Another function of the editorial assistant is answering phones for editors and shielding them from pitches by would-be authors. Rayanna Simons served a stint as a first reader at the adult trade book division of Macmillan. She recalls one memorable conversation:[2]

> Caller: *Do you publish books?*
> Reader: *Yes.*
> Caller: *I'm a manic–depressive.*
> Reader: *Oh. Have you written a book?*
> Caller: *No. I've been too depressed. But they're changing my medication.*

Clearly, not all would-be authors are crazies and not all raw submissions are rubbish for the slush heap.

◆ Author contact: At college, when you dreamed about becoming an editor at a large publishing house, a concomitant benefit was the opportunity to develop close relationships with famous authors. At lunch at the Four Seasons with Anne Rice (you paid with your company credit card), you would exchange pungent patter while deftly probing about her next book and how many millions she was going to ask for as an advance.

Well, this may be a future reality, but as an editorial assistant your author contact could be limited to greeting Ms. Rice in the company's reception area and leading her back to your senior editor's office. If she gets to know your name, she might call you often, but only to complain about not receiving her royalty check or reviews on time.

◆ Checking the competition: When a new book is under consideration at a publisher, a basic practice is to check all books on the same subject. This is accomplished by scanning *Books in Print*, where books are listed by topic and author. The editorial assistant may also be asked to provide a summary of any book of a similar nature.

The editorial assistant will also visit large bookstores to check current books to see how they match up against a proposed book. One former editorial assistant was researching a proposed book on résumé preparation. The author had hyped its uniqueness. When the editorial assistant visited the bookstores, however, he found sixty-five books on job hunting, many of which had lengthy sections on résumés.

◆ Attending editorial meetings: Publishing companies have frequent meetings, and the editorial assistant is often asked to attend—usually to take notes or minutes of the meeting. Don't fret. What may seem tiresome at the time will prove to be an essential stage in the learning experience.

◆ Handling department's clerical work and filing: In addition to answering the phone for an industrious senior editor, the editorial assistant is also called on to retype, sort, and log manuscripts; run off duplicate manuscripts on a high-speed copier; and type jacket and catalog copy. The editorial assistant performs all these functions for a small remuneration. The average salary is from $17,000 to $24,000, but bear in mind that it's only a starting point in the fascinating world of books.

Editorial positions (not described) and their salary ranges.

Executive Editor, College Division: $45,000 to $64,000

Executive Editor, Elhi Division: $61,000 to $83,000

Acquiring Editor, College Division: $33,000 to $41,000

Developmental Editor, College Division: $27,000 to $34,000

Senior Editor, Juvenile Division: $35,000 to $40,000

Assistant Editor, Juvenile Division: $19,000 to $21,000

Qualifications for General Editorial Positions

A college education is a must. A passion for reading and for the touch, smell, and feel of books is a prerequisite. The would-be book publishing professional must also have a thorough understanding of grammar and current English usage. Proficiency in typing and/or word processing is also helpful. A special knowledge of a particular field or discipline such as science fiction, history and politics, and fiction in trade publishing, or perhaps of math or science in textbook publishing, may accelerate promotion. Sometimes textbook editors are former schoolteachers. Often, journalism majors go into book publishing, creating a more competitive field.

The opportunity to work with books is most appealing, yet, as we have already seen, the salary ranges in book publishing are low. The fringe benefits, however, of day-to-day contact with creative, interesting co-workers, the occasional contact with well-known authors and celebrities (although this is the exception rather than the rule), and just the chance to be involved with the wonderful craft of books may make the financial sacrifice worthwhile.

Production Jobs

Production Director/Vice President Production: The production director determines specifications and production processes for the publishing unit and establishes overall production department plans and roles. This individual hires and trains production supervisors, art directors, and estimators; and coordinates and schedules elements of the editorial and production process. In addition to procuring raw materials, he or she assures quality of printing, maintains schedules, and oversees the adherence to budgets. The production director maintains relations with suppliers, purchases production-related goods and services, and oversees suppliers' fulfillment of quality, cost, and schedule obligations. The salary range is from $50,000 to $123,000.

Production Supervisor: The production supervisor analyzes and consults with editors on specifications for paper, cloth, binding, typography, and reproduction processes. He or she secures estimates based on project specifications and selects vendors. The salary range is from $50,000 to $66,000.

Interview

In an interview in Image World, *Stephani Hughes, former production supervisor at Simon & Schuster, discusses her job function.*

As production supervisor, I manage many steps of the book production process, all the way from manuscript to printing. The pace is fast. You have to be very organized and detail-oriented to succeed in this business.

For each book, the first thing I do is assign the design work to a freelance artist. When the design is approved, the manuscript is sent to a typesetter, and then we paste up the mechanicals in-house. I deal with at least five companies that handle the printing and binding of the inside pages. The book jackets and covers are handled by four or five other printers. When the book goes to press, I have to be there to OK the press sheet. The greatest satisfaction is the finished product. You have a book that you can hold in your hands.

I was a business major at Ferris State College. Many of the people I work with are English majors, some have degrees in printing.

Cost Estimator/Production Estimator: The cost estimator provides cost estimates to production management by obtaining actual current costs from vendors of all production services and materials. He or she also maintains contacts and understanding of traditional and new graphic arts processes and costs. The salary range is from $22,000 to $30,000.

Art Director/Design Director: The art director establishes overall artistic guidelines, themes, and quality control standards. Responsibilities include the hiring and training of staff, recruitment of freelance resources, assignment of work on projects, including design of covers, jackets, and packaging, and supervision of the creative staff output. The art director sets and approves budgets and schedules, approves costs and bills for design and art, and maintains quality and artistic merit based on understanding of the market, competition, usage requirements, and the like. The salary range is from $47,000 to $55,000.

Artist/Designer: The designer understands editorial, marketing, and production requirements of a particular book and provides a design theme and artwork that meet these requirements. The designer is also responsible for selecting the typefaces and type size for the book, choice of display type, and dimensions of the page elements. He or she keeps to a schedule that meets the financial and deadline requirements of the project. The salary range is from $25,000 to $40,000.

Production Assistant: This is an entry-level position. The production assistant secures estimates and submits them to the production manager for evaluation and analysis. He or she coordinates movement of the manuscript to the compositor by assisting in the development of the schedule, by trafficking of the galley proofs and page proofs, and follows up with suppliers. The salary range is from $14,000 to $18,000.

General Qualifications for Production and Art Positions

Production people are in charge of the physical design and manufacture of books. A thorough background in typography, printing processes, paper manufacturing, art and graphic design, and mathematics is necessary for these job functions. Although there are many fine art schools, there are few specializing in printing processes.

Computerization and desktop publishing (DTP) has revolutionized book and magazine publishing, replacing the traditional methods of typesetting, pasteup, and sometimes even printing. Gaining a knowledge of desktop techniques is essential for a career in production. Many courses in DTP are offered by college extension divisions. There are also many fine publications, including *Publish!*, servicing this market.

Salaries in this field are not high and are generally less than at advertising agencies. Often the work pace of meeting deadlines is feverish. There is great satisfaction, however, when the book is completed and meets the industry's high standards.

Marketing

The book is the ultimate editorial product, and it is this product that the marketing people must sell to bookstores, supermarkets, drugstores, libraries, schools, colleges, and, finally, to the reader/consumer. Here are the people who make this happen.

Marketing Director/Vice President Marketing: The marketing director develops marketing objectives, policies, and strategies, as well as marketing plans by product and market. He or she identifies marketing capability for present and future products, spots trends, and integrates market research and product development information. The marketing director hires and trains in-house and field staff in order to develop an efficient and effective organizational structure. The marketing director maintains good communications with the marketing and editorial departments, and evaluates the effectiveness of editorial and marketing strategies, participates in forecasting and budgets, and is responsible for meeting sales and expense budgets. He or she also controls inventory levels. The salary range is from $92,000 to $125,000.

Sales Manager: The sales manager plans sales forecasting and oversees the sales force. He or she recruits, trains, and motivates sales representatives, conducts sales meetings, and assigns territories. The sales manager is responsible for developing budgets and forecasts, new product introduction, sales activity, and field reports. He or she supervises or influences the creation of book jackets and makes recommendations on the development of promotional materials. The sales manager makes personal contacts with major bookstore chains. The salary range is from $51,000 to $75,000.

Direct-Mail Manager: The direct-mail manager analyzes markets for books and selects appropriate lists to reach those markets. He or she supervises or prepares copy for brochures and sales letters; directs and supervises all graphics for direct-mail pieces; and oversees accurate record-keeping of all sales resulting from direct-mail efforts. The salary range is from $28,000 to $48,000.

Sales Representative: The sales representative calls on bookstores, libraries, schools, and colleges, in order to take or stimulate orders; and turns in market research data and editorial from the "field." He or she also attends sales and training meetings. The salary range starts at $19,000 for beginners and goes up, depending on experience, territory, and sales record.

Advertising Manager: The advertising manager researches markets and available media, prepares and submits the advertising budget, and recruits and trains copywriters, artists, and traffic managers. He or she establishes a relationship with an advertising agency or in-house advertising department; organizes advertising schedules; and determines books to be advertised, medium and space to be used, deadlines, and cost. The advertising manager originates cooperative advertising ventures with dealers and monitors actual ad placement, responses, performance of media, and follow-up sales. The salary range is from $39,000 to $61,000.

Promotion Manager/Sales Promotion Manager/Promotion Specialist: The promotion manager schedules advertising, direct mail, exhibits, and other promotional activities. He or she recruits and trains staff and assigns work to staff and outside agencies. The promotion manager reviews industry reports and written and visual material. He or she consults on catalogues, in-store displays and other sales tools, maintains contact with the advertising agency and media, and directs selling by coupon and other direct-response advertising. The salary range is from $39,000 to $61,000.

Publicity Director/Publicity Manager: The publicity director compiles lists of appropriate sources of book reviews for each title published and places review copies with all appropriate sources. He or she prepares publicity releases and stories on authors and their books and distributes them to appropriate newspapers, magazines, TV programs, columnists, and so on. The publicity director plans authors' parties; organizes authors' tours around the country; and maintains clippings files of reviews and other press coverage given to books and authors. The salary range is from $43,000 to $80,000.

Subsidiary Rights Director/Manager: The subsidiary rights manager keeps close communications with the editorial department. He or she markets the licensing of rights to others to use the firm's published materials, including book club distribution and translations; foreign publishing; mass-market reprints; publication in newspaper and periodicals; performance on the broadcast media; and quotation in anthologies and other publications. He or she consults regularly with the marketing manager concerning subsidiary goals and follows up each sale of subsidiary rights. The salary range begins at $28,000 and goes up to $60,000 and more, depending on the size of the publishing house and the degree of responsibility.

Copywriter: The copywriter develops schedules for copy development. He or she obtains information about books from the editorial and marketing departments. The copywriter writes basic cover and other copy and develops variations. The salary range is from $17,000 to $27,000.

Marketing Assistant: This is an entry-level position. The marketing assistant maintains sales records, distributes review copies of books, and assists in the preparation of catalogs and in the writing of specialized promotion pieces. The salary range is from $19,000 to $22,000.

Marketing positions (not described) and their salary ranges

Regional Sales Manager: $28,000 to $47,000

International Sales Manager: $36,000 to $55,000

Book club positions (not described) and their salary ranges

General Manager: $68,000 to $108,000

Editor: $34,000 to $40,000

General Qualifications for Marketing Positions

As with magazines, the best editorial product in book publishing will also fall on its face if it is not distributed and marketed efficiently. The marketing people are the shock troops. They do battle with wholesalers, retailers, distributors, and college professors, their basic objective being the selling of books. Often it's not fun, but it can be financially rewarding and a source of great pride in accomplishment when a line sells well.

One needs a marketing personality to sell used cars or aluminum siding—aggressive, outgoing, persuasive, and charming. A book is a different kind of product. A book salesperson, visiting the head of the psychology department at a university, needs a keen understanding of his book as well as its subject in order to persuade the professor to adopt the text for her classes.

Similarly, the sales manager for a large publisher must be conversant with the themes of her entire seasonal line, which may number a hundred books. Add intelligence and a love of reading to the other qualifications, and you have a book marketer.

Job Shifting in Book Publishing

As in most fields, particularly in the media and communications professions, job shifting in book publishing is a way of life. People move upward within their own company or by taking jobs at other publishers.

A regular feature in *Publishers Weekly* called "People" reports these changes. Readers may find this column useful in defining upward mobility in book publishing. Here are some examples:

> *Gilly Hailparn named publicity manager Avon books. She was associate director of publicity at Bantam Books.*

> *Anne Yarowsky appointed senior editor in illustrated books department of S&S. She previously directed Yellow Press, her own company.*

> *Paul Farrell named editor-in-chief of Henry Holt's computer book group. He was formerly an editor at John Wiley.*

Susan Dalsimer named VP of publishing for Miramax Books, an imprint of Disney's Hyperion Books, launched in 1994. She previously worked for Warner Bros., acquiring books for films.

Mark Ciccone named VP merchandising Bantam Doubleday Dell. He was with Procter & Gamble.

Joan Schulhafer has been named director of publicity at Avon Books. She was an independent consultant.

Minorities and Book Publishing

African Americans, Hispanics, and Asians are as underrepresented in book publishing as they are in other communications professions. In terms of officials and managers, which includes executives in all phases of publishing, African Americans account for only 4 percent, while Hispanics and Asians account for about 2.6 percent in total. Even in office and technical jobs, the three minorities account for only about 20 percent.

Under the leadership of the Association of American Publishers (AAP), book publishers are moving aggressively to improve representation by minorities. The problem lies in misconceptions about the industry's requirements. For one, the notion exists that only English majors need apply. Publishing, the AAP maintains, is a business that needs people with accounting, law, production, public relations, and data processing skills. By offering scholarships and conducting an informational campaign, it is hoped that minorities will be attracted to book publishing.

The Range of Entry-Level Jobs

We have given some examples of entry-level jobs available in publishing. Here are some additional beginning jobs:

Accounting clerk

Assistant in subsidiary rights

Clerk-typist
College sales representative
Customer service representative
Mail room clerk
Manuscript traffic clerk
Production assistant
Proofreader
Publicity assistant
Reference library assistant
Secretary to an officer

Of course, job availability will limit your choices. Land the job, then you can widen your options.

Notes

1. "Getting Into Book Publishing," The Association of American Publishers, 1992.

2. Rayanna Simons, "Slush," in *Editors on Editing,* ed. Gerald Gross (New York: Harper & Row, 1985).

Chapter 7

◆

The Making of a Book from Creation to Publication

I n chapter 4 we discussed the structure of book publishing, describing the roles of all the individuals and organizations contributing to the book publishing process. In succeeding chapters we will offer a closer look at the departments within a publishing company and their roles in creating and marketing books.

In this chapter, we follow the creation of a hypothetical book of fiction, from the author's conception to its appearance on the bookstore shelf, and beyond.

The Submission Period

Let's suppose that our would-be author is a tenured professor of humanities at a small midwestern college. He has already published his doctoral thesis and numerous articles in professional journals.

He has never published fiction. Now he is writing his first novel, which takes place in post–World War II Germany, a period and place of special interest to him.

Since his proposal has already been turned down at his own university press, and realizing that most fiction is placed with publishers through literary agents, the professor begins a solicitation of thirty agents, sending them each a ten-page outline of the novel, his bio (brief autobiographical sketch), his dissertation, and reprints of some of his articles.

After months with no success, an agent from New York, whom the professor had met briefly at a professional conference, expresses interest in the book. The agent suggests a meeting in New York (at the professor's expense), where the project can be discussed more fully. During lunch at the Algonquin Hotel, a celebrated authors' hangout, the agent confirms to the professor that she thinks she can sell the book, but will need to see certain changes in the outline that will make the book more salable to the publisher. The professor disagrees in principle, but finally agrees to submit a revised outline in a few weeks.

About a month after the agent's receipt of the revised outline, the professor receives a call from her with the good news that a major trade book publisher is very interested in the book but wants to see two completed chapters before making a commitment. The professor is reluctant to comply without a contract but agrees when the agent says that it's common practice.

Because the professor had done several rough drafts of the whole book a year before these discussions, it takes him only a few months to complete the chapters. The publisher reads the chapters, is impressed with the quality, and agrees to publish the book on the next year's fall list, which will give the professor about fourteen months to write the book.

(A few words about lists and seasons: Most publishers have three principal seasons—winter, spring/summer, and fall—when they issue catalogs showing their "list." The list includes some of the publisher's list of books already in print—the backlist—as well as its forthcoming titles for that season—the frontlist. The frontlist, of course, receives greater emphasis.)

Before a decision can be made on a submission, the project must first be approved by the publisher (the titular editorial head of the company) and by other editorial and marketing brass. Any strong negative arguments, such as poor sales of similar novels, can kill a book proposal. In this case, the publisher's enthusiasm for the plot and the professor's fluid writing style win out.

The agent handles the deal with the publisher's acquisition editor, and after some negotiation, they agree to an advance of $8,000, half on signing and half on completion of the accepted manuscript, a respectable figure for a first-time novelist. The author idealized an advance of $25,000, but this was not to be.

One must understand the precariousness of publishing a work of fiction, particularly one by a new author. In a given year, American publishing houses put out more than three thousand new fiction titles to a booksellers' market that can't absorb that many works. Further, much of what sells is commercial "good read" fiction of the Judith Krantz, Jackie Collins, and Sidney Sheldon variety. Literary fiction, such as the professor's book, appeals to a much smaller market.

After the agent and the publishing house's editor-in-chief have agreed on all points and a contract has been signed, the professor is invited to New York to meet with the publisher's staff on procedures, coordination, scheduling, a possible author's tour, and similar details.

The Author Meets the Publisher

At his visit to the publishing house, consisting of a two-hour lunch with his assigned editor and a few hours chatting with other people, the author is a bit disappointed. Somehow he thought his book would be greeted with more fanfare, more enthusiasm. He is, however, impressed with his own editor, who conveys the feeling that the book will be a success if the style, tone, and pace of the first chapters carry through. She is the author's primary contact throughout the writing stage.

The author/editor relationship is key to the writing process, with the editor assuming many roles. At various times, she may goad, cajole, question, and praise. Often the simple comment, "What do you really mean?" or "You can do better than that" may be all that's needed to shore up a shaky section. The editor's firm hand-holding is particularly important when working with a first-time novelist.

In our hypothetical situation, the professor goes home and settles down to the meticulous and rigorous task of writing the book. As with most authors, there are infertile periods and many distractions, but with stamina and self-discipline, the professor perseveres, and fifteen months after his meetings in New York, he submits the first of several drafts of the manuscript.

When the manuscript is finally accepted, the laborious regimen of development and copyediting begin at the publishing house. After being read for content, the manuscript is checked and rechecked for style, usage, grammar, and punctuation. When this process is completed, the manuscript is ready for typesetting, the first stage in the manufacturing process.

The Marketing Stage

During the editing period, the editorial and marketing people have been meeting to plan the marketing campaign for this book and others on their fall list. Catalogs for the trade are being printed. On the strength of what the marketing people have seen of this novel, they budget a paltry $15,000 for a marketing campaign and agree to a ten thousand-copy first printing. The campaign will include small ads in the *Village Voice Literary Supplement* and in a half-dozen literary journals. The publicity department plans a four-city author's tour.

When the professor/author first visited the publisher, he met with the promotion and publicity managers who learned that the author had been in military government, stationed in Germany, after World War II. The book will be somewhat autobiographical, as are many first novels.

The central character of the novel is an American military governor who becomes involved with a half-Jewish German woman who was able to survive the Holocaust by hiding her true identity. The emotional aspect and the author's involvement are deemed to be sufficient ammunition for a promotional thrust.

However, the publisher will not commit to best-seller promotion until there are favorable reviews and good early sales results. The book receives only a quarter-page in the publisher's spring catalog, not indicative of a great deal of optimism. One positive factor—the marketing people have come up with a new catchy title that should bolster its sales. The author shudders at the new title, but as a first-time novelist, he is not given a choice.

While the book is being copyedited, the design team at the publisher has been making decisions on the book's typeface, page layouts, and the artwork for the cover. The company's publisher and editor-in-chief approve the design, but it is not shown to the author until it is a fait accompli.

As soon as the cover is color-proofed, a simulated book is prepared. It consists of bound type galleys with a cover wraparound. The galleys are the complete text of the book, but are usually uncorrected at this time. Bound galleys are sent to reviewers early enough to make their deadlines. They are also sent to other authors and celebrities, inviting testimonials that can be used on the book's back cover and for promotional purposes.

The subsidiary rights people submit the bound galleys to the major book clubs. Although the two largest clubs, Book-of-the-Month and Literary Guild, do not buy it, a small scholarly club elects to make the book its principal monthly selection. Book club selection conveys prestige to a book and is a definite advantage in promoting sales.

The book goes to press about three months before its publication date, allowing adequate time for it to be distributed to wholesalers and bookstores.

When the first books come off the press and are delivered to the publisher, most of the staff agrees that it is indeed an accomplished novel, one destined for success. The editor-in-chief and the author's editor send him special congratulatory notes. At this point, general good feeling abounds.

Meanwhile, the author begins preparation for his tour. Although a practiced speaker, he is tense about the media interviews.

The book receives mixed reviews. It doesn't make *The New York Times Book Review*, but the *Village Voice* review says it is "marked by extraordinary psychological insight." A review in the *Los Angeles Times* refers to the author as "an emerging talent." Still another review says that the author "writes in the shadow of Saul Bellow." In general, the reviews are optimistic, but not the stuff that makes books run off the shelves.

The Tour

The author begins his tour. As an unknown, he must establish rapport with the interviewers. Unfortunately, he finds himself saying the same thing to three or four interviewers in the same city. The rigors of traveling and interviews prove exhausting. He is further frustrated when he appears at book signings and only a few dozen people show up. The author complains to his editor about the poor promotion, but to no avail. Particularly distressing is the sight of a book superstore not stocking the book.

The subsidiary rights manager makes a pitch to the major movie studios for possible movie rights. She is unsuccessful, being told generally that the story is not high-concept enough to make a movie.

Foreign sales rights are pursued early in the process of a book's publication. Large publishers maintain ongoing relationships with certain publishers in foreign countries that receive first refusal on a publisher's properties.

In our hypothetical situation, a major publisher in Germany buys the rights for a $4,000 advance and a six-thousand-copy first hardbound printing. Of course, the story takes place in Germany, which explains the interest. Publishers in other countries take a wait-and-see attitude by passing on the rights until the book has a U.S. sales history.

The subsidiary rights people are not too disappointed because the book will be on sale for a few months by the time the Frankfurt Book Fair begins in October. Then, if the book is successful in the States, there will be dozens of opportunities for foreign rights sales.

The Aftermath

When all the returns from bookstores are taken, the book sells about seven thousand copies, the rest are to be remaindered. Remainders are unsold books disposed of by a publisher below cost to bookstores that, in turn, offer them for sale to their customers at a fraction of the book's original price. The book never goes to paperback and is not optioned as a movie.

Here is the story of a potential bestseller—at least in the author's mind—but it doesn't happen. The book is well written, but perhaps the publisher didn't support it enough. In fairness to the publisher, however, this novel is just another piece of literary fiction that is difficult to propel to the top. In the end, the publishing house doesn't quite make back its expenses on the book. Other than his advance, the author/professor receives no additional income. He returns to the serenity of academia somewhat disillusioned. He is not prepared to accept that only a few dozen of the three thousand novels published each year make the best-seller list. Or, in another sense, only an insignificant number of authors get rich from their craft.

After initial disappointment, the professor begins thinking about his next novel, this one about a lusty, fortyish English professor and her affair with a twenty-year-old track star. Maybe this one will make it.

The Travails of a Real-Life Author/Professor

Like the professor in our first scenario, Robert Olen Butler suffered the anguish of rejection as an author of fiction. However, Butler attained glorious success, winning a Pulitzer Prize in 1992 with the publication of his seventh book, *A Good Scent From a Strange Mountain*, stories of Vietnamese émigrés living in Louisiana.

An article in *Publishers Weekly (PW)* tells of Butler's tortuous path to this coveted award.[1] Beginning in the 1980s, Butler published six novels that sold poorly, although they achieved critical success.

During this period he changed agents, editors, and publishers a number of times until he finally landed on the friendly terrain of Henry Holt, which published *A Good Scent* in 1992.

To promote the book, Holt sent the author on a three-week coast-to-coast tour that included interviews as well as bookstore readings. A reader, Charles Johnson, who turned out to be a Pulitzer Prize juror, missed the reading in his local bookstore, but was so impressed with the work, he furthered it in the Pulitzer proceedings.

In 1994, Holt published Butler's *They Whisper*, a lyrically beautiful narration of the nature of sexual intimacy. For this book, the publisher sent Butler on a fifteen-city reading tour.

Ultimately, Butler succeeded brilliantly because he found the right publisher and, more important, he writes about subjects he knows. A Vietnamese war veteran, Butler now teaches fiction writing at McNeese State University in Lake Charles, Louisiana. This area has been a haven for many Vietnamese refugees, the people he writes about in *A Good Scent From a Strange Mountain*.

Butler says that he is "life-drunk," a condition that should give him material for many books in the future.

Notes

1. Sybil S. Steinberg, "Robert Olen Butler," *Publishers Weekly* (January 10, 1994): 67.

Chapter 8

◆

How a Trade Book Publisher Acquires Books

I n writing about the selection process and how a publisher puts together its lists of new books, I am reminded of a comment attributed to Barry Diller, former C.E.O. of Paramount and 20th Century-Fox Pictures. Diller is supposed to have said, "If I made every picture I turned down, and turned down every picture I made, over a three- or four-year period, I would be in the same place."

Roger Straus, long-time head of Farrar, Straus & Giroux, is widely known in book circles as a man of taste and intuition. Under his aegis, since its founding in 1946, Farrar, Straus has published such literary giants as T. S. Eliot, Bernard Malamud, Alexandr Solzhenitsyn, and, more recently, Susan Sontag, Philip Roth, Joseph Brodsky, and Carlos Fuentes.

But even the sagacious Straus has had his share of misjudgments. Offered a chance to be the first American publisher of the novelist Umberto Eco, he chose instead another obscure Italian author. Eco's

The Name of the Rose went on to sell more than three hundred thousand copies in hardcover for another publisher, and his later work *Foucault's Pendulum* enjoyed similar success.

Which books to publish is a publisher's most significant decision. Yet much of this process is merely intellectual guesswork. The problem is also magnified when the publisher is committed to a list of as many as 100 to 150 books a year. In this chapter, we focus on the members of the selection team and their considerations in structuring a list.

Interview

In May 1995, we discussed the role of an acquisitions editor with Eugene (Gene) Brissie, who has performed this significant function for more than twenty years.

Gene Brissie is a native New Yorker. He attended the Lawrenceville School and was graduated from Princeton University. Brissie started his career in the Subsidiary Rights Department at Farrar, Straus & Giroux, eventually becoming director of foreign rights.

After four years, he left Farrar, Straus for the Pocket Books division of Simon & Schuster, where he started the Subsidiary Rights Department. A few years later, Brissie became editor-in-chief of Pocket Books's trade paperback imprint, as well as vice president and, ultimately, associate publisher of Fireside Books, Simon & Schuster's largest trade paperback imprint.

In 1984, Brissie joined the Putnam Publishing Group, where he was named vice president and publisher of Perigee Books, remaining in that position for more than eight years. From 1992 until 1995, he was vice president and executive editor of Chicago-based Contemporary Books. In 1995, he returned to Simon & Schuster as vice president and editorial director of business and self-improvement books in the Prentice Hall division.

You have been an editor for at least the fifteen years that I have known you. Can you trace your career path, including your major at college and first job, which trained you for the position you now hold?

I majored in English and American Literature at Princeton and worked for a couple of summers at Harcourt, Brace. My first job out of college was a brief stint as a copy editor for a very small publisher. My first real job was at Farrar, Straus & Giroux. In my subsequent years at Pocket Books and Simon & Schuster, I was either editor-in-chief or associate publisher of three different imprints.

My training was definitely "on the job." It strikes me that anything you do in this business is good training to be an editor or, ultimately, a publisher. Selling foreign and domestic rights made me a much better editor than I would otherwise have been. One of the things you do all day long is sell, sell, sell—to an editorial board, to an author, to publicists, to sales reps, and so on.

I think it helps to be willing to take the next, logical step in any job. I suppose I tried to do things that were in addition to those comprising my job. As a subsidiary rights assistant, I was willing to help someone in the department send out books or manuscripts or make follow-up calls, which eventually led to making the deals themselves. Once you take all those other steps, it is a very short time before you close a deal. Once you close a couple of deals, you quickly do more.

It also helped to have bosses who expected and encouraged me to keep doing more. The same was true in making the transition to editor. When I was selling rights, I also tried to bring in a couple of books. Once I brought in a couple, it was easy to bring in more. At some point, I had a boss who said, "Why don't you become an editor?" It goes back to my point that any job you do in the industry helps you to become a better editor, if that is what you want to be. The jump to editor-in-chief or publisher takes place with time and experience. At some point you realize that you know how to handle lots of different books and lots of different authors and perhaps other elements of the business, such as marketing.

As the editorial director of a division within a large publishing company, do you operate autonomously from your parent publisher, or if you do interact with them, what form does this take?

I do not operate completely autonomously, although there is a certain amount of freedom. I answer to the president, I buy books via an editorial board, and I am constantly getting advice from our marketers and the sales manager; if they cannot sell what I buy, there is no point to the exercise.

How much of your time is spent on acquisitions and how much on editing?

I do spend a lot of time acquiring books—and overseeing editors who also do so—and a good deal less time editing. Much of that gets done by the editors who work for me.

Do the literary agents present their best book ideas to a number of editors simultaneously, or do they single out editors with whom they have close personal and business relationships?

There are agents who submit only to multiple editors, and there are agents who submit selectively, and there are some who do a little of both.

How does an editor cultivate the top agents?

See them; take them to lunch; respond in a timely fashion to their submissions and, for heaven's sake, return their phone calls.

When working with celebrity authors, is it almost always necessary to hire a ghostwriter to work with these authors?

Not always, although it is most of the time.

How are these ghosts compensated, and do they receive a share of the author's royalty?

A ghost, in my experience, gets a piece of the advance, although not necessarily any of the royalties. Some ghosts, however, are worth half the advance and royalties, the maximum that can be expected.

How many books do you have in process at any one time?

We publish about seventy-five business and self-improvement titles per year. I personally work on perhaps five to ten.

Are there any areas of book publishing that do not seem to be getting their share of bright young talent?

I do not think so. There are so many bright people coming into the business and looking for any opportunity to get into it that I don't think any areas are being ignored. Sometimes, aspiring editors make the mistake of thinking that the only way to become an editor is to become an editorial assistant first. As I mentioned previously, in my experience, everything you do in the business—promotion, subsidiary rights, publicity, sales—helps make you a better editor.

Is book publishing, once past the entry level, as poorly paid as has been suggested, and does the compensation structure equal the other areas of mass communication once one reaches the middle-executive level and beyond?

There is no question that the pay at entry level is low. Compensation gets much better at the middle levels and above. It is certainly competitive with advertising and newspaper and magazine publishing; I'm not familiar with compensation in TV and radio.

What college training would you recommend for those seeking to make book publishing their life's work?

Mostly, read everything you can get your hands on, whatever the subject. Make books a part of your life and reading second nature. That is more important than majoring in English or liberal arts or business. The people who do best in this business are the people who read and love books, whether the format be print or electronic.

Is there really any opportunity to be published for the writer without an agent? What would you suggest?

Yes, we publish a number of writers without agents. That said, an agent is definitely the path of choice for a previously unpublished writer. A lot of agents will evaluate over-the-transom [unsolicited] manuscripts or proposals. They also scour magazines for interesting new writers, so doing pieces for periodicals is sometimes a good way to get an agent or book contract. Writers should write and publish wherever they can.

The Editorial Acquisition Players

At a publishing company, the responsibility for acquiring books lies with the publisher at the top, and, on a day-to-day basis, with the editor-in-chief, assisted by senior editors and procurement and executive editors. We refer to this group generically as acquisitions editors. In addition to this team, when a major book property becomes available and a large advance is called for, the president and the head of the house are consulted.

Often, the editor-in-chief is the leading player in the acquisitions game. To perform the job effectively, an editor-in-chief must possess a broad range of taste that encompasses such varied subjects as pop culture as well as popular science and politics. If the house publishes fiction, the editor-in-chief and her staff must have an acute sense of style and the ability to evaluate good writing by merely scanning a few pages of a manuscript.

The editor-in-chief must also be willing to gamble on unpublished authors who show potential, even if it means a great deal of hand-holding throughout the writing period. The job, however, does not end with the writing. Often, editors are integrally involved in the marketing of books they have acquired for publication.

In addition to acquisition chores, the senior editor's job often includes the editing of a dozen or more books in one year.

The size of the acquisitions team varies with the size of the house and the number of new books it publishes yearly. At Simon & Schuster's trade book division, there are thirteen individuals with the rank of senior editor and above, all of whom are concerned with acquisitions. At a smaller house, Farrar, Straus & Giroux, about ten people bear the responsibility of acquiring the roughly two hundred new books it publishes annually. William Morrow & Company publishes almost five hundred new books a year, split up into seven different lines. About twenty people at this house put together the company's diverse list.

How Books Are Acquired

There are more than a dozen sources for procuring the books that make up a publisher's list. We will discuss a number of these.

Raw Submissions: Few publishing houses today accept unsolicited manuscripts, sometimes known as "slush" or "over the transom." Publishers have generally found that it is too costly to handle these submissions. Publishers will either return an unsolicited manuscript to the author unread, with a polite note stating the company's policy or, in many cases, not return it at all.

Nevertheless, each year a number of unsolicited works are published and become successful. A simple word of advice to authors without agents. Before sending a manuscript to a publisher, inquire about its policy on submissions.

Literary Agents: Most of the books that ultimately reach the exalted position of appearing on a publisher's list come from agents. Agents pre-screen manuscripts and thereby perform a service for publishers. As a result of their contacts, agents are in the best position to place a property at the right house.

Agents represent established authors, since many authors do not have exclusive publishing arrangements. Acquisitions editors for trade houses spend a great deal of time negotiating and interacting with literary agents for the works of established authors. Literary agents also conduct auctions on behalf of name authors' books that are deemed to have mass-market appeal.

Prospecting: In the late 1970s, I taught a course on magazine publishing at New York University. An enterprising acquisitions editor at Prentice-Hall, Mary Kennan, contacted me about writing a book on magazine publishing. I agreed to do the book, *The Magazine*, which has been in continuous publication since 1979. Editors regularly scan catalogs of college extension and continuing education programs for provocative subjects for books that might be written by the individuals teaching the courses.

Other acquisitions editors peruse newspapers and magazines for subject ideas and potential authors. Contacts with theatrical agents also turn up celebrity clients who may be persuaded to become authors. Where a ghostwriter is required for one of these projects, both publishers and literary agents maintain a roster of competent writers.

Writers' Conferences: Literary agents frequently attend the major writers' conferences. When convenient, acquisitions editors attend them as well, with the objective of discovering promising writing talent. Literary magazines have also proven a productive source for finding new writers.

Foreign Translations: Publishers are often given the opportunity to publish the English-language version of a book first published in another language. Many American publishers attend the Frankfurt Book Fair each October, where thousands of books in every language are made available for translation purposes. Competition is often feverish for the big books with a track record, published abroad.

Rotten Rejections

In publishing, stories abound about "the big one that got away." In the book *Rotten Rejections*, publisher Bill Henderson has collected the rejection notices of some famous works that were originally turned down by publishers before they were ultimately accepted.[1]

MADAME BOVARY

Gustave Flaubert (1856)

You have buried your novel underneath a heap of details which are well done but utterly superfluous.

CATCH-22

Joseph Heller (1961)

I haven't really the foggiest idea about what the man is trying to say.

THE SPY WHO CAME IN FROM THE COLD

John le Carré (1963)

You're welcome to le Carré—he hasn't got any future.

THE DEER PARK

Norman Mailer (1955)

This will set publishing back twenty-five years.

THE TIME MACHINE

H. G. Wells (1895)

It is not interesting enough for the general reader and not thorough enough for the scientific reader.

RUDYARD KIPLING (1889)

I'm sorry, Mr. Kipling, but you just don't know how to use the English language.

(Editor of the *San Francisco Examiner* informing Kipling, who had had one article published in the newspaper, that he needn't bother submitting a second)

JONATHAN LIVINGSTON SEAGULL

Richard Bach (1972)

Jonathan Livingston Seagull *will never make it as a paperback.*

(James Galton, publisher of *Modern Library,* refusing an offer from Macmillan to bid on the paperback rights to Richard Bach's best-selling novel. Avon Books sold almost eight million copies of the book.)

Steps in Buying a Book

Excluding the big book from a name author that is acquired by auction or through negotiations with a literary agent, most publishers follow a meticulous procedure in acquiring a book.

As a matter of policy, weekly editorial meetings concerned with acquisitions and works in progress are held. These meetings are attended by the editor-in-chief, senior and executive editors, and assistants. A procurement, or acquisitions, editor who wishes to pitch a submission or an idea for a book, will generally circulate the proposal in advance of the meeting. If she or he has the support of two or three editors, it will make the selling job easier.

At the meeting itself, a book proposal is accompanied by an editorial evaluation of the manuscript summarizing its theme, the author's previous work, his or her background, and the book's promotional possibilities. Other key matters discussed are marketability, how many books have been written on the same subject, and how they have fared.

If the group present at the editorial meeting judges a book proposal worthy of further consideration, the publisher and editor-in-chief may request a detailed outline from the author, especially if the book is nonfiction. If it is a piece of fiction, they may wish to read the author's previous work, and either a few chapters or the entire manuscript of the proposed work.

At the same time, the senior or acquisitions editor will prepare a cost analysis for the book and determine the number of pages it is expected to be and the estimated number of copies to be printed. These numbers are weighed against the book's projected sales to arrive at a break-even point.

After all the editorial and financial criteria have been met, and the editorial board gives the green light to the project, the acquiring editor begins negotiations with the author or his/her agent concerning the size of the cash advance against future royalties, when the advance is payable, the delivery date, the royalty percentage, and the sharing of subsidiary rights.

Once there is agreement on these terms, a contract is prepared by the editor with the aid of the publisher's legal staff. When this stage is completed, the acquisitions editor often brings the author in to meet the firm's publisher, top editors, and marketing, public relations, and promotion people. These meetings are extremely important, particularly for the author, who then begins to feel that he or she is a part of the publishing family.

What is the acquisition editor's role during the writing and editing stage? Often, the editor who buys a book will also edit it, at least in the developmental and line editing phase; that is, everything but copyediting and proofreading. The editor is also involved in the design of the cover and inside pages, works with the company's marketing and promotion staff, and may even write catalog copy and plan an author's tour.

When a book is completed, its editor has performed a Sisyphean task. It is a job she will repeat more than a dozen times a year in the high-anxiety atmosphere of acquiring and editing books.

Notes

1. Andre Bernard, ed., *Rotten Rejections* (New York: W. W. Norton & Company, 1990).

Chapter 9

———————◆———————

The Nuts and Bolts: Copyediting, Design, and Production

When the author submits his or her completed manuscript to the publisher, it then flows through the production pipeline. First, it must be line edited and copyedited so that it is in the proper literary form to go to the printer. Then, a designer or art director designs the physical aspects of the book. An in-house or outside typesetter sets the type, which is then printed and bound into a complete book.

Copyediting

In an interview, a veteran production editor made these comments on the craft of copyediting:

> *It does take a compulsiveness ... a person who isn't compulsive isn't going to catch all the typos, or care,*

or worry about whether a word is spelled right or
whether a phrase is as clear as it should be.[1]

What makes a good copy editor? A love of books and the English language is a basic quality, as is respect for authors and what they are trying to accomplish. The copy editor must be an expert on words, grammar, and usage, and also possess a keen eye for detail.

The copy editor's job begins when the senior or general editor has already done the "creative," or developmental, line editing. He or she then pores over the manuscript, as a kind of word inspector, searching for errors in spelling, punctuation, and grammar, and seeking out inconsistencies and repetitions.

The copy editor must also be aware of the nuances of language. He or she attempts to eliminate jargon from a manuscript and avoid pretentious language. Although the copy editor does not function as a co-author or researcher, he or she may be asked to cut portions of the manuscript, a very sensitive task.

Most publishing houses spare the copy editor the tedium of fact-checking, especially since the workload of an in-house copy editor may include as many as twenty-five manuscripts at a time.

The copy editor marks a manuscript alongside the words in question, or when there is a query for the author or editor, places a colored paper flag at the margin. An example: The copy editor may also make margin notations stating, "Awk" (awkward) or "Meaning?" Since these little love notes are often anathema to authors, tact is essential in fulfilling the copy editor's role.

If convenient, at most publishing houses a meeting is set up between the copy editor and the author before the type is set. When this procedure is completed, the manuscript goes to the production editor, who prepares it for typesetting. When the galleys (proofs) come back from the typesetter, the copy editor (and the author) checks them carefully.

Monitoring this whole procedure is the managing editor, who acts as a traffic cop, keeping the words moving smoothly and on schedule, and acting as a general troubleshooter, especially when a manuscript is late.

Copyediting by a Pen-driven Computer

In the not-too-long ago, copy editors labored over their manuscripts using colored pencils and pens to convey their numerous corrections of an author's manuscript. Later, when authors began transmitting their manuscripts to publishers on a computer floppy disk, copy editors looked at the pages on a computer screen while making changes on the keyboard.

Enter the PenEdit system. An article in *Publishers Weekly* tells of a progressive new development in computer-driven copyediting.[2] Using an electric pen, the copy editor can "write" the corrections and suggested changes on a pen-driven computer. The manuscript on the disk is altered accordingly. It is then sent to the author for comments and corrections.

In 1993, Viking Press, an early user of the pen-driven computer, copyedited the mystery book *Hardscape* on the PenEdit system. At the time of this writing, many other publishers are using this innovative development.

The Art of Book Design

The practice of designing books goes back to the time of illustrated bibles and predates early developments in typesetting and printing. Many famous artists in the post-Renaissance period illustrated books. It has always been a tradition in publishing that good design sells books.

Think about the elements of a book's design. For our example, we choose a work of hardbound fiction or nonfiction. Typically, in the production of such a book, two designers are involved: the principal book designer and the designer of the book's jacket. These decisions are based on budgetary considerations and are made in consultation with the publisher, the book's editor, and the production department.

The Role of the Book Designer

Here are the assignments of the principal designer:

♦ the selection of the paper stock for the dust jacket (book jacket), the cover book cloth, the endpapers, and the text

♦ the choice of typeface and spacing for text and headlines

♦ the design of the title page

♦ the selection of the display initial and chapter number that begins each chapter

♦ the style and design of the cover and spine stamping, if any

♦ the staining of the book pages for decorative effect, if any

♦ the commissioning of the author's photograph for the back of the dust jacket.

Only a small fraction of the total number of books in a bookstore are displayed full face. Obviously, for those books the cover presents a unique selling opportunity.

There are many options for the design team. Should a photo or illustration be used, or will an all-type approach be more effective? Has the author's previous book or books established him or her to a wide audience, so that the name on the cover is as important as the title? Will embossing on the cover enhance the book's image? By past experience, what colors work best? And, finally, what typeface will best convey the image and subject matter of the book? These and other questions challenge the designer.

Consider the field of children's book illustration. The well-executed children's book provides a magical world of fantasy for its young readers. The designer works with the editor in pairing an accomplished team of author and illustrator. Seldom do authors of children's books illustrate them. Since children's book illustration is such a competitive field, the design/editor team has a vast choice of diverse talents from which to make their decision.

For children's book illustration assignments the artist's portfolio must show a consistent vision so that an editor can follow the direction the artist has taken and match him or her with the right author.

Design and illustration are integral to the production of textbooks, many of which are elaborately designed. Most medical books use a profusion of color photographs and illustrations. For a medical illustrator, training may include years of observation in surgical and clinical procedures at hospitals and medical schools.

In the field of mass-market paperbacks, the designer has fewer options. Within the front and back covers of this $5^1/_4$-by-8-inch product, the designer must sell the image of the book in a front-cover illustration or type, and use the back cover for a synopsis, blurbs, and the author's background.

To perform these significant tasks, publishers often use freelance designers for the overall book design, and call upon other freelance specialists to handle the book jacket.

Artists and Illustrators

A commercial artist may be a magazine illustrator, the production designer and art director of a film, the visual artist for a TV production, or a book designer and illustrator. All are basically artists, whose talents give aesthetic character to their media.

Illustration plays a major role in textbooks. A friend of mine is a well-known medical illustrator. Her detailed, graphically incisive color illustrations are used in many medical journals and textbooks. Integral to her work is a profound understanding of the human body and its functions.

Most books are not illustrated; therefore, the artist's role may be that of illustrating only the dust jacket or cover. This is nonetheless an important assignment, as the appeal of a jacket on the bookshelf increases the book's sale. (Some books merely have black-and-white line illustrations inside, but they, too, can play a vital role in a book's presentation.)

In addition, an artist can be a book designer. A designer may select the typeface for the body text and headings, design the jacket, and/or assign the illustrations for the jacket and the inside of the book. The book designer may also be involved in the selection of paper to be used as well as the fabric for the cover.

The reader interested in commercial art is urged to read the Society of Illustrators' wonderful annual awards book. In it, there are awards given for excellence in magazines, advertising, institutional publications, and books. The works of the winners in the book category truly exemplify the significance of art in books. If you can't find this volume locally, write the Society of Illustrators at 128 East 63rd Street, New York, NY 10021.

How A Book Is Produced

The purpose of this section is not to train readers as production people, but rather to orient them in the various phases of the production process of a book. Within the limitations of this chapter, however we will present some basics.

Typesetting

For more than four hundred years after Gutenberg's invention of movable type, all type was set by hand, a tedious process. Each letter or character was a separate piece, made at first of wood and later of metal. In 1886, typesetting was revolutionized by Ottmar Mergenthaler's invention of the Linotype. Now, for the first time, a full "line of type," in one piece of metal, or "slug," could be set by machine.

In the Linotype system, which held sway for newspapers, magazines, and books until the 1950s, the operator typed out the copy on a keyboard. The machine arranged matrices (individual type molds) into a line of words. When a line was completed, the machine delivered the metal slugs. For books that were typeset on the Linotype, these metal slugs were collected on a metal tray, called a *galley*, which was then inked to pull *galley proofs*.

There are hundreds of different typefaces, divided into two basic styles: *roman* (straight up and down) and *italic* (slanted). Most faces come in both roman and italic. Type is further classified by its breakdown into *serif* (letters that have fine lines finishing off the main strokes) and *sans serif* (letters with no such fine lines). Type is further delineated between *bold, medium*, or *light face*. Many typefaces that were designed more than two hundred years ago are still in use today.

Typefaces are designed to serve the imagination of the designer or art director who may choose from a wide variety of available faces.

Today, the somewhat primitive Linotype has given way to photo-typesetting. Modern computer technology produces about fifteen hundred characters a minute, or ninety thousand characters an hour, without sacrificing quality. Desktop computers are used in page lay-out and proofing, as well as for typesetting.

Printing

There are three printing systems in use today: *letterpress, gravure,* and *offset. Letterpress* is the oldest, dating from eleventh-century China.

In letterpress, printing is by the raised, or *relief*, method. For short runs, sheet-fed presses are used, for longer runs, web-fed rotary presses print from rolls.

Gravure uses a sunken, or *depressed,* surface for the image. When gravure printing is done on a rotary press, the process is called *roto-gravure.* Gravure printing offers a greater variety of shadings from light to dark than is possible with the other two printing systems. However, this system is seldom used in book printing, since its economy is only effected in very large runs.

Offset lithography is a method of printing from a flat surface. It is the most-used process for book printing. There are offset presses for short, medium, and long runs. Both sheets and rolls are used, depending on the capability of the presses.

The major advantage of the offset process is the simplicity of preparation, since no expensive molded or cast plates are required.

The Desktop Revolution

Computerized desktop equipment at a publishing house allows for high speed in the typesetting process. It also affords the designer the opportunity of experimenting with dozens of typefaces in a variety of sizes on his or her desktop. Type can be bent, expanded, toned, even placed on curves.

For books that involve color photographs or illustrations, desk-top equipment like the Macintosh, a color scanner, and software separate the subjects into four-color film negatives. This work may be done inexpensively in-house, or farmed out to service bureaus. Color correcting is also done electronically before the pages go to press.

Most design schools are emphasizing desktop publishing (DTP) training. Their graduates have a head start in entering the field, needing only on-the-job training on specific functions.

Paper

Paper for book production comes in different weights, shades, degrees of opacity, and texture. For mass-market paperbacks, publishers use inexpensive, groundwood paper, which is off-white in color, and is usually supplied in rolls designed for high-speed offset presses.

For limited-run trade, technical, or textbook publishing, the more expensive "free" (free of groundwood) papers are used. These papers are generally bulkier than groundwood, and are bleached to ensure permanency. The quality of a book's paper is an important factor in its overall presentation.

Most hardbound books have coated, or "slick" paper dustcovers, which have display value and also serve as protective jackets or wrappers.

Binding

Binding refers to the finishing process after a book is printed. Some printers have their own binderies, other binders are located separately.

There are two basic binding processes used in book production: *Smyth-sewing* and *perfect*. The printer may supply the unfolded sheets to the binder as they come off the press, or fold the sheets into eight-, sixteen-, or thirty-two-page "signatures," or sections, as part of the printing press's operation. The signatures are then gathered together, along with the covers, and bound.

In Smyth-sewing, an expensive process, a special sewing machine threads the pages of each signature, and all the signatures together, in preparation for receiving the cover.

If the book is to be "case-bound," the cover is composed of a leather, leatherette, or plastic fabric wrapped around stiff boards. Endpapers are then attached to the insides of the cover and adhered to the first and last pages of the body of the book.

Many books, especially mass-market paperbacks, are "perfect-bound." In this process the sections are held together by a flexible adhesive. The cover is glued on to the body, and the backbone is square, giving a neat, attractive appearance to the book.

Copyediting, design, and production offer challenging careers. All three of these areas are creative and make an important contribution to the book publishing process.

Notes

1. David Frederickson, "Manuscript Connoisseur," *American Bookseller* (April 1990): 72.

2. Paul Hilts, ed., "I Sing the Editor Electric," *Publishers Weekly* (January 3, 1994): 43.

Chapter 10

◆

How Publishers Handle
Publicity and Promotion

Among the divisions of HarperCollins, a large publishing house, are HarperPerennial, HarperBusiness, HarperCollins Trade, Interactive, and Harper San Francisco. To introduce its line of books for Spring/Summer 1995, the publisher ran a sixteen-page ad in *Publishers Weekly*'s January 2, 1995, issue. The ad featured sixty-three books, each of which received promotion, publicity, or advertising. That's how trade books are sold in today's competitive market. Here are some examples from this catalog:

- ◆ Barbara Taylor Bradford, *Dangerous to Know*

  500,000-copy first printing

  12-city National Author Tour

  $300,000 National Marketing Campaign

  National Advertising in *New York Times Book Review*

- ◆ Ken Blanchard and Don Shula, *Everyone's a Coach*

  250,000-copy first printing

TV and Radio Satellite Tour

6-City National Author Tour

12-Copy Floor Display

◆ Rodney Dangerfield, *No Respect*

200,000-copy first printing

Radio Advertising in Major Markets

8-copy Counter Display

◆ Leon Uris, *Redemption*

350,000-copy first printing

Syndicated Radio Interview

10-City National Author Tour

Foreign Rights Sold in the U.K., Germany, Finland, Spain, Latin America, Mexico

◆ Margaret Thatcher, *The Path to Power*

250,000-copy first printing

National Advertising in *New York Times Book Review* and six other newspaper review sections

6-City National Author Tour

Alternate Selection of the Book-of-the-Month Club

9-Copy Floor Display

Barbara Taylor Bradford is a best-selling author whose nine previous novels have gained an international following for her. Don Shula is a winning pro football coach. His book is about inspirational and motivational management techniques. Rodney Dangerfield is the noted comic. Margaret Thatcher, Britain's former prime minister, has written one previous best-seller. Leon Uris's bestseller *Trinity* sold eight million copies. All five authors are well-known personalities, yet all agreed to submit to the rigors of promotions and publicity tours.

The Elements of Book Promotion and Publicity

In promoting a book, the publisher uses advertising judiciously, primarily because it is expensive. The cost of a full-page ad in the book review section of *The New York Times* is about $19,000. Unless the ad is accompanied by a coupon, the response to such advertising is not measurable. Why, then, do publishers use advertising in book promotion?

The answers are many. With name authors like Jackie Collins, whose books consistently make the best-seller list, the publisher's commitment to advertising is contracted. With other important authors, the publisher engages in some subtle ego stroking when it runs ads for their books.

Ads in book review sections are read avidly by bookstore owners and librarians, who may order books in anticipation of buyer and reader demand.

Book advertising is also aimed at wholesalers and distributors, who are thus alerted to the possibility of a book taking off as a best-seller.

Finally, an ad for a book reaches the consumer, who is motivated to buy it based on the copy in the ad and the blurbs from critics and notables.

The Author's Tour

Author's tours are the sine qua non of book promotion. Simon & Schuster used tours for about one-third of the books in its winter 1995 catalog.

Much has been written about the rigors of author's tours. Husband-and-wife authors Michael Dorris and Louise Erdrich are veterans of the tour wars. Dorris characterizes a day on the tour: "You begin the day a starry-eyed, energetic self-promoter ... and end ready for a straitjacket."[1]

On a multicity tour, appearing on dozens of radio call-in shows, on television, and in bookstores, Dorris said he feels like:

> ... *a badminton birdie batted back and forth across the skyline of Denver or Boston or Chicago. One stop you're the jovial raconteur, an anecdote a minute; the next you're Mr. or Ms. National Public Radio, serious and literary. You're self-deprecating in talking to a newspaper reporter, aggressive on a phoner (call-in show), defensive, trusting, joking, serious. You take on the mood of your interviewer, the colors of your context.*[2]

What does an author do on a tour or promotional junket, as they are sometimes officially characterized? Here is a list of the major elements of a tour:

♦ National and local television talk shows

♦ Call-in radio shows

♦ Newspaper and magazine interviews

♦ Bookstore readings and signings

♦ Meet-the-author luncheons

Book Signings

Book signings are an important component of an author's tour. The *Los Angeles Times* Sunday Book Review section lists the forthcoming week's book signings. For the most part they are well attended and contribute to a book's sales. In one week noted there were twenty signings and in another a half-dozen authors reading from their works.

These events must be carefully planned and promoted, otherwise they may prove embarrassing and frustrating to the author. For the bookstore, autographed copies may sell well, even after the author goes on his or her way, especially if the author is a celebrity.

How HarperCollins Spent $200,000 to Promote a Book

Book promotion budgets rarely exceed $100,000, even for celebrity authors or those with a proven sales record. In April 1995, HarperCollins committed $200,000 to promote and advertise psychologist John Gray's *Mars and Venus in the Bedroom: A Guide to Lasting Romance and Passion*. Gray's *Men Are from Mars, Women Are from Venus* was a *New York Times* best-seller that sold three million copies, and his *What Your Mother Couldn't Tell You and Your Father Didn't Know* was also a best-seller.

Here's how this publisher spent its big bucks on Gray's book:

♦ 750,000-copy first printing

♦ $200,000 national marketing campaign

♦ Network cable television advertising

♦ 10-city national author tour

♦ 12-copy floor display

♦ HarperAudio tie-in

♦ A main selection of the Literary Guild

This lavish promotion had other beneficial effects for the publisher. Not only did it build up the author's stature to a mass audience, but also set up a very large sale when the book went to paperback.

What does the author talk about on such an extensive campaign? Gray's subject matter leaves him no shortage of provocative topics. His book tells "what turns men on" and, of course, "what turns women on," as well as "how can a long-time monogamous couple make sex new again."

Book Parties

Book parties provide free food and drink and often a heady mix of glitz and glamour. The book party phenomenon is significant in a book's promotion. In fact, on occasion *Publishers Weekly* has devoted space to these events. At times the guest list for these parties may number in the hundreds. One objective for the publicity people planning these parties is to invite celebrities. Often these are friends of the author, as well as other writers on the publisher's roster.

Why, one may ask, does the publisher run the expense of these parties? Book parties may serve as a pay-off to the author. Also, they help create a buzz in the industry about the book's importance. Finally, since press people attend these parties, there is often coverage in the celebrity columns. Do the parties help sell books? The answer would have to be, maybe.

Other Book Promotion Techniques

Today's book promotion people have stretched their skills and imagination to a degree of sophistication beyond the limits of even ten years ago. In January 1994, Simon & Schuster published Helen Thayer's *Polar Dream,* about a solo journey of a woman and her dog to the North Pole. Thayer was accompanied on her eight-city author's tour by her loyal husky, Charlie.

In promoting a cookbook, the publisher ran a cross-promotion with a major food company, which included supermarket tie-ins and inserts in suburban newspapers.

To promote a garden book a publisher conducted press receptions for garden writers and reviewers.

Publishers often tie in elaborate promotions to the industry's annual ABA convention. Here, publishers reach the book trade in a receptive setting.

When a book is developed into a movie, TV show, or miniseries, there are numerous opportunities for cross-promotion. Just the line at the bottom of the movie ad, "From the novel ───," is worth additional sales of the book. Bookstores will often cooperate in these efforts by displaying the book prominently.

Point-of-sale displays in bookstores have always been strong promotional tools. Of course, these are expensive and require bookstore cooperation. The stores must order a quantity of a single book and devote space for the display.

The Benefits of Book Promotion and Publicity

In an article in *Publishers Weekly,* Thomas Weyr sheds light on book promotion and publicity: "Although book publicity and promotion is still an inexact science," says Weyr, "there are accepted norms in its practice, and unanimity in its necessity."[3]

Leigh Haber, publicity director of Harcourt Brace Jovanovich, states it positively: "Publicity used to be the icing on the cake; now it is far more significant. It can make or break a book."

The multimedia aspect of book promotion is clearly a positive factor. Books are reviewed in thousands of newspapers and magazines. They are "talked about" in these media as well. Not a day goes by where an author is not plugging his or her book on the network morning talk shows.

Authors appear regularly on the syndicated shows *Donahue, Geraldo,* and *Oprah.* These shows can "make" a nonfiction book. One publicity director claims that an author's appearance on *Oprah* can sell as many as thirty thousand books.

Cable, too, is a player in the book publicity game. ESPN works well for sports books, and CNBC is a good showcase for business books.

Do all new books receive the publicity treatment? Weyr's *PW* article includes an informal survey. At Putnam, 60 percent get some form of promotion. Random House does something for each book on its list, as does Little, Brown. Macmillan estimates that 50 percent of its books get more than routine publicity, and 25 percent of its authors are toured. Crown, a division of Random House, publishes five hundred books a year and tours about 20 percent of its authors.

Getting Hired in Book Publicity

Publicity staffs at publishing houses are not large. At HarperCollins, the staff numbers seventeen, at Putnam twenty-three, Simon & Schuster fifteen, and Random House eleven, plus six show-bookers on the West Coast. Most other large houses have about ten people in their publicity departments.

What qualities do publishing companies look for in publicity candidates? A number of qualities surface in Weyr's article: style and flair, enthusiasm, organization, savvy, flexibility, sense of humor, creativity, love of books, and college paper experience. One should also have secretarial skills, and, once hired, be prepared to spend much busy time on the phone booking interviews.

Notes

1. Michael Dorris, "Ode to an Author Escort," *Publishers Weekly* (June 7, 1991): 34.

2. Ibid.

3. Thomas Weyr, "Publicity's New Punch," *Publishers Weekly* (November 16, 1990): 15.

Chapter 11

◆

The Fascinating World of Subsidiary Rights

In 1994, Chuck Hogan, age twenty-six, had been working in a Boston video store for eight years when his first novel, *The Stand-off*, was bought by a major publisher for more than half a million dollars.

The paperback rights were sold for a similar sum and, later, a major Hollywood studio bought film rights and assigned Hogan to write the screenplay. Translation rights in French, German, Dutch, Italian, Spanish, and Portuguese were sold to publishers in those countries. These are just a few examples of how subsidiary rights were used for this fortunate young writer.

The Elements of Subsidiary Rights

By definition, subsidiary rights are the rights to the use of a book in ways other than original publication. The purpose of subsidiary rights is to serve as an ancillary source of profits, beyond the original publishing of a book. The subsidiary rights pie can be sliced into a dozen pieces. Here are descriptions of the individual elements.

Reprint Rights

Paperbacks are considered reprints, although in the strictest sense a reprint can be a new edition in the original hardcover format. When a trade publisher publishes a book with the potential of being issued at a later date in a cheaper paperback edition, it will either negotiate separately with one paperback publisher, or offer the property simultaneously to a number of publishers in an auction.

At auctions, millions of dollars may be bid for the paperback rights to best-selling hardcover works of fiction and nonfiction. Sometimes the original publisher of the hardcover edition and the paperback publisher will work together on a book project from its inception. In such a situation, they will share in paying the author's advance; share promotion and printing costs; and share the proceeds in proportion to their revenues.

In selling reprint rights, the hardcover publisher uses the original manuscript or advance proofs in its solicitation, rather than waiting for a completed book. For most trade publishers, selling reprint rights is the most significant area of subsidiary rights.

Foreign Rights

In a large city in central Germany, on the Main River, more than eight thousand publishers from ninety nations and sixty thousand professionals convene for the book industry's annual Frankfurt Book Fair. Their principal purpose is the buying and selling of book rights.

At that giant annual convocation, the world's publishers meet to buy and sell rights. In a recent high-powered deal, the American publishers of the author Tom Clancy sold the world Spanish rights to his next novel for $600,000 to the large German publisher Bertelsmann's Spanish division. But not all rights sales are in that league. The newly emerging Eastern European publishers buy rights for advances that are as little as $1,000.

A major American publisher, HarperCollins, may send as many as twenty-five of its executives from various divisions to Frankfurt each year to sell rights to its book properties. A hot book by a name author is often sold to a dozen or more different countries.

Publishers often sell foreign rights to a book before its original edition is published. There is a gamble, of course. If a book achieves best-seller status, and the publisher holds off on rights sales, it will be worth that much more in the after market. In either case, however, agreement is made at the time of the sale over when foreign editions will be published.

Large publishers do not wait a whole year till the Frankfurt Book Fair to negotiate foreign rights sales. Many foreign publishers employ scouts in the United States who report to them on what is currently being published, trends, and future hot properties. Also, the subsidiary rights department at a large publisher maintains constant contact with foreign publishers over rights sales.

Not only fiction and nonfiction trade book publishers sell foreign rights. Textbooks, children's books, and scientific and reference works also have an active foreign sales market.

At Frankfurt, an American publisher may also purchase the American or English-language rights to a book published in another language. At times, co-editions are arranged, whereby a joint printing in a number of languages is effected.

Typically, the originating publisher controls and shares in subsidiary rights with the author. However, some authors control their own rights. An author I know had a novel published in 1993 in the United States by a major publisher. His contract with that publisher gave him ownership of foreign rights. As a result, there was a U.K. and French edition published at the same time the U.S. edition was published. Of course, in such a situation, the author receives a smaller advance from the U.S. publisher. This author, incidentally, controlled his own movie and paperback reprint rights.

There are other book fairs where rights are exchanged. The London Book Fair is held each year in March for the sale and exchange of rights. The leading market for children's books is the annual

Bologna Children's Book Fair, held in April. Both fairs are conducted primarily for the sale of rights.

Movie and Television Rights

When John Grisham's best-selling 1991 novel, *The Firm*, was made into a big-budget movie, millions of dollars changed hands. Publishers work very closely with movie and TV producers on the sale of rights to books they publish. The major movie studios see most promising manuscripts before they are published. Not only is a great deal of money involved, but also a book's sales are enhanced when the publisher can announce that the book is soon to be a major movie or TV miniseries.

Often, when a movie is made from a book, a special paperback tie-in book is published at the time of the movie's release. Also, when a movie from a book is a hit, the author's previous works enjoy renewed success. The leading Hollywood talent agencies, ICM, CAA, and William Morris, maintain active literary departments for the purpose of selling books they represent for motion picture and television production. Often, these sales are made in conjunction with other literary agents.

Book Clubs

The sale of a book club edition falls into the domain of subsidiary rights. There are more than two hundred book clubs. As a group, they account for about 5 percent of all publishers' net book sales. The largest club, the Book-of-the-Month Club, has more than two million members.

When a publisher makes a deal with a book club, it gives the club a set of the book's printing plates, and the club prints its own edition. At times, the book club prints along with the publisher to cut costs. Club members receive the book at a discount. The publisher receives approximately 10 percent of the club's price for each book printed. The author also receives a lower royalty on these sales. The prestige of being a book club selection can significantly help a book's sales in bookstores.

For major trade books, book club auctions are held. In 1992, the Literary Guild, another large book club, guaranteed an advance of

$460,000 for the rights to Nelson DeMille's *The General's Daughter*, published by Warner Books. The publisher's subsidiary rights director conducted the auction.

Magazine and Newspaper Prepublication and Postpublication Rights

A publisher may sell the rights to a chapter or a portion of a book to a magazine or newspaper before or after a book's publication. Although this is not a major revenue source, there is promotional value for a book that is excerpted in a large-circulation publication. There have been situations where an entire book was serialized after its original publication.

Interview

Kristin Kliemann has a B.A. in English and sociology from Trinity University in San Antonio, Texas. Upon graduation in 1979, she attended the Summer Publishing Institute at Rice University in Houston. Within weeks, she left for New York City to seek a job in publishing. Her first position was as an assistant in the subsidiary rights department at Harcourt Brace Jovanovich. After eighteen months there, she left to become associate director of rights at Farrar, Straus & Giroux. Two years later she left Farrar, Straus for what turned out to be only one year at Holt, Rinehart and Winston as rights manager. She then returned to Farrar, Straus as director of subsidiary rights and eventually vice president. In 1991, Kliemann left Farrar, Straus again for her current job as subsidiary rights director of Hyperion/Disney Press, which is a book publishing operation owned by the Walt Disney Company. Kliemann teaches at various summer publishing programs and in the continuing education division of New York University. She lives in Hastings-on-Hudson with her husband and son.

If you had your education to do over again, how would you change it considering your present career?

I have a B.A. in English and sociology, which, perhaps contrary to what is expected, has served me well in my career. The English (both literature and practical writing skills) has helped in that I am at least somewhat aware of the world's "great books" (which helps in evaluating just where a given new title fits into the spectrum). And I learned how to write a sentence/essay/thesis, which, I'll admit, over the years has been boiled down to knowing how to write a decent pitch letter.

Now that's not to say that I couldn't use a bit more education. If I had the time, I'd definitely invest in an M.B.A. The publishing business is rather peculiar as businesses go: fully returnable goods, relatively low margins, no tradition of market research, very little product identity in the marketplace, etc. I have the impression that a broader knowledge of general business practices and marketing possibilities would be very useful.

At Hyperion, what is your most profitable source of subsidiary rights?

Subsidiary rights income is shared between the publishing house and the author, and the splits on the shares are determined by the contract between the author and the publishing house. Generally book club rights are split on a fifty-fifty basis (many other subsidiary rights are split significantly in the favor of the author), so licensing book club rights is one of the areas that is most profitable for us.

Focus on a specific book you published in the last few years and go through all the subsidiary rights sales generated by this book.

A few years ago, we published a book called *Outsmarting the Female Fat Cell* by Debra Waterhouse. The book is about diet and nutrition and why women always lose weight more slowly than men. Six months after publication we had more than a hundred thousand copies of the book in print. It made a few best-seller lists and the following rights were sold:

- First serial to *Good Housekeeping Magazine*: This excerpt (which was mentioned on the cover) appeared just as the books were landing in bookstores around the country.

- Book club rights: Both Book-of-the-Month Club and Literary Guild were interested from the time they first saw the manuscript. (I submitted the book approximately nine months before our publication.) After six rounds of bidding, rights went to the Literary Guild. We also licensed rights to Better Homes and Gardens Book Club and Rodale Book Club.

- Paperback reprint rights: We originally acquired that title in an auction with other publishers. And when we won, one of the other players decided they would at least get in on the book by trying for paperback rights. They called immediately and offered us a "floor" bid (the lowest bid acceptable) of $20,000, which we accepted. However, after we published the book, the final deal was considerably more than the $20,000 we started with.

- Second serial: We had a bonanza of postpublication serializations on this title: The *New York Post* and the *Los Angeles Times Syndicate* decided to pick up a three-part excerpt to offer to its subscribers. In addition, various monthly magazines picked up pieces: *The Globe, Women's Health Letter, Your Health Magazine,* and *New Body Magazine.*

- Foreign: The author's agent controlled these rights, and she licensed rights to a publisher in England (where the book was a best-seller). The book also appeared in French, German, Italian, and Swedish.

Describe Hyperion's coverage of the Frankfurt Book Fair and what subsidiary rights sales you expect from this source.

For American publishers, the Frankfurt Book Fair is a chance to license foreign rights—English language rights to non–U.S. publishers and translation rights to publishers around the world. Most of August and September is spent getting ready for this week in October. We send copies of all the books published since the last fair and we prepare fairly complete lists of the books we plan to publish over the next few seasons. We prepare a list of books to discuss with subagents and foreign publishers. Over the five days at the fair, I meet with nearly a hundred different people. I discuss current books as well as proposals for future titles.

I always hope to make sales at the fair. For the most part, though, since the fax machine has made doing worldwide business so manageable, I use the Frankfurt Book Fair as a way to see people face-to-face and gather a bit of extra information about what kind of books might be of interest in a particular market or to a particular editor. Then I hope that over the six months following the fair I'll be able to reap the rewards and make some licenses on my titles.

How can people break into subsidiary rights?

The easiest and probably the most typical way to break into subsidiary rights is to come to New York as a young college graduate and take an entry-level position in a rights department. I have, perhaps twice in the fifteen years I've been in rights departments, known people to come into rights from other avenues—generally from the marketing area of publishing. In order to "make it" in rights at any level, one must have at least some of the following skills/characteristics: good copywriting skills, good negotiating skills, and a familiarity with publishing contracts and the rights marketplace. It also helps to have a sense of humor and inherent need to have fifteen different projects happening simultaneously.

Paul Nathan's Column

Paul Nathan's excellent column, "Rights," appears in each issue of *Publishers Weekly*. One recent column had a fascinating piece on iconoclastic author Frederick Lenz III.

Snowboard Guru

Frederick Lenz III has a Ph.D. in English Literature, teaches computer programming, owns several advanced technology companies, and holds a seventh degree black belt in karate. In 1985 Fawcett published his Lifetimes: True Accounts of Reincarnation, *now in its 15th printing.*

Recently, on his own, he brought out Surfing in the Himalayas, *which deals with the fast-growing sport of snowboarding from a Buddhist point of view. Rather than sell copies, Lenz has been giving them away. One ended up in the hands of agent Nicholas Ellison. Confident that the book had the bestseller potential of* Zen and the Art of Motorcycle Maintenance, *Ellison obtained more copies and sent them around to New York houses for an auction.*

Before that came off, an offer was received from Germany, thanks to an alert international scout, and Goldmann clinched the rights for $100,000. Shortly thereafter, the domestic auction was over; Mel Parker took the book for Warner at $250,000. Since then Hodder & Stoughton has closed for U.K. rights, Sperling and Kupfer for Italian, and Distribuidora Record, Brazilian. Book-of-the-Month and Quality Paperback have just acquired club rights.[1]

Nathan's column is typically spiced with provocative bons mots on the subsidiary rights business. Reading Nathan provides a liberal education in this area of publishing.

C A R E E R   T I P

There are not many subsidiary rights jobs in book publishing. Even large publishers do not maintain large staffs in this specialty. One breaks in as an assistant and moves up the ladder. A firm's subsidiary rights director typically has vice presidential status, with salary and perks commensurate with that office.

Note

1. Paul Nathan, "Rights," *Publishers Weekly,* May 15, 1995: 18

Chapter 12

◆

From Concept to Bound Book: The Role of Book Producers

An enterprising book producer, Steven Ettlinger, several years ago conceived the idea of doing a book on tools and hardware stores for do-it-yourselfers. Ettlinger spent two years researching the subject and actually writing the book. He then wrote a sample book proposal, which he pitched to many publishers. After a series of rejections, Macmillan bought Ettlinger's idea, *The Complete Illustrated Guide to Everything Sold in Hardware Stores*. It went on to sell more than fifty thousand copies. On a consumer guide such as this one, Ettlinger associates himself with an expert in the field and hires researchers to help him assemble vast quantities of basic information. He then writes the book, or CD-ROM, from this pool of resources. He directs the research, writing, illustration, and production, and acts as agent for all of his projects. He has also produced *Don't Pick Up the Baby or You'll Spoil the Child & Other Old Wives Tales About Pregnancy, The Nitpickers Guide For Next Generation Trekkers*, and about a dozen others.

In chapter 4, "How Book Publishing Is Structured," we gave a capsule description of the function of book producers, formerly known as book packagers. Let's discuss their role in greater detail.

For the publisher, dealing with book producers builds in cost controls not always possible when books are produced in-house. When the publishing company contracts for a book with a book producer, it knows its costs up front. A publisher might, for example, issue an order to a book producer for twenty-five thousand copies of an illustrated book at $9 each. The publisher will have established in advance all the standards for the book in terms of editorial and production quality and approve the elements of the book at various stages, but its own efforts are reduced primarily to marketing.

Arrangements with producers vary. At times, the book producer's contract will call for delivering camera-ready pages to the publisher, which in turn will arrange for printing and binding the book; at other times the producer supplies finished books. Often the publisher comes up with the concept and turns it over to the book producer for execution. In many cases, however, the producer acts as an agent for the writing of the book. In such a situation, the book producer receives an advance against royalties, plus an agreed fee for editing and writing services.

Paul Fargis, another book producer, was responsible for the second edition of the best-selling *New York Public Library Desk Reference*. The giant compendium of the most-asked questions at the library was published in 1993 by Prentice Hall. He was also chosen to manage the revision of Doubleday's *Made Simple* books, a forty-five-title series.

In recent years, book producers have produced such successful titles as:

The Joy of Sex
The Hite Report
What They Don't Teach You at Harvard Business School
Imagine: John Lennon
Rolling Stone Photographs
Ben and Jerry's Homemade Ice Cream and Dessert Book

The Best of Gourmet
Jim Henson's Bedtime Stories
Born to Shop (11-book series)
Reader's Digest Creative Cooking Club

Such major publishers as Little, Brown; Doubleday; Simon & Schuster; Allyn & Bacon; Crown; Harcourt Brace Jovanovich; William Morrow; and Macmillan are active users of book producers.

In 1980, the American Book Producers Association was formed to further the interests of its book producer members. Today, the group has seventy members. If you are a freelancer, you may be listed on their freelancer database by writing to them at American Book Producers Association, 160 Fifth Avenue, New York, NY 10010; (212) 645-2368, Fax: (212) 989-7542.

There are today more than two hundred book producers in the United States and Canada. They account for more than one in eight published books and are certainly considered a growth area in publishing.

Chapter 13

◆

The Business Side of Publishing

Yes, it is the publisher and the acquisitions editors who have a regular table at New York's Four Seasons restaurant, but it is the business side that keeps the spokes on the wheel. The business side is responsible for the budget, accounting, payment of authors' royalties, shipping, and maintaining the warehouse and inventory controls.

Of course, the size of a publishing house determines the extent of its business side. A multidivision firm may have divisional presidents and staffs who, in turn, report to a group or corporate president, who reports to a CEO and board of directors. In a small firm, just a few people make up the management structure.

The business side operates very much like any other manufacturing organization except that in publishing there is a creative product—books. The publisher must install a system that has adequate resources to meet the payroll, give advances and royalties to authors, manufacture books, store and ship them to wholesalers, book chains, and retailers, and collect the monies due.

Today, most of these functions are computerized, which allows for greater efficiency, but doesn't necessarily speed up the inflow of money. Collection is the publisher's greatest woe. Many large chains do not render prompt payment for the books they order, since most are overextended themselves. Even college bookstores and state agencies are in the slow-pay category. When more money goes out than comes in, the publisher must resort to borrowing and with it, the cost of debt service.

Returns are a common problem for publishers. Mass-market paperbacks are almost always sold on consignment, and if sales run less than 50 percent of distribution, the publisher must account for this waste in its profit structure. Sales of hardcover trade books are usually sold on a return basis, so that books may sit on racks in a bookstore for more than a month, and then be returned for full credit. In recent years, the publishing industry has amended its returns practices.

Where the Book Dollars Go

Let's say you bought a popular novel at a neighborhood bookstore for $23.50, its list price. Of course, if you bought the same book at a superstore you might have received a 15 percent discount. However, for the purpose of our example, we'll deal with the $23.50 price. An article in the *Los Angeles Times* details who gets what of the price you paid for the book.[1]

Bookseller	$11.28
Publisher	4.93
Paper, printing, and binding	3.06
Author	2.00
Promotion	1.88
Agent	.35

As we can see, the largest share goes to the bookseller. Yet this share is obviously reduced when a book is heavily discounted. The publisher, however, must meet its payroll and fulfill all its financial goals, including profits, on a smaller slice of the pie. That doesn't allow for much margin for error.

The largest items on a publisher's balance sheet are paper, printing, and binding, factors that run about one-third of a company's gross sales revenues. The bottom line for a publisher with gross sales of about $20 million may be no more than 4 percent, which doesn't allow for much margin for error.

The business side of publishing is less glamorous than the editorial side, but its smooth functioning is vital to a firm's operations.

Note

1 Josh Getlin, "Art and Science of Book Pricing," *Los Angeles Times,* October 9, 1994, p. 14.

Part III

The Wide Range of Trade Publishing Activity

Chapter 14

◆

The Popular World of General Trade Books: Hardcover

Let's define the word *trade* as it relates to book publishing. Trade books are books of general interest sold to individual readers in bookstores. The category also relates to books borrowed from libraries. Trade has two subcategories: general trade books in hardcover and trade paperback books. Each of these categories has about 650 publishers. Some are small, publishing fewer than a dozen titles each year; others are large companies, often owned by conglomerates.

The trade category is further subdivided into adult and juvenile. Adult trade is, of course, the larger of the two categories. To illustrate this wide range, we list below a number of books from a recent Simon & Schuster trade books catalog and, alongside each title, we designate its classification:

Passion, Profit, and Power	Self-help
Memory's Ghost	Psychology
Dead by Sunset	True Crime
Clash of Titans	Military History
Gentle Discipline	Child Care and Family
CodeName Downfall	History
The Slightly Older Guy	Humor
Eating Well Is the Best Revenge	Cooking
The Blood Countess	Fiction
From Chaos to Confidence	Business
Beyond Dreams and Beasts	Computers
Nightingales' Song	Politics
Darwin's Dangerous Idea	Science
Golf Is Not a Game of Perfect	Golf
Repair and Improvement	Home Improvement
Angel Encounters	Inspiration
Love, Miracles, and Animal Healing	Pets
The Joy of Grandparenting	Gift
Divided Lives	Women's Studies

Publishers list a book's classification below its description in their catalogs as a guide to booksellers and libraries. In a large bookstore, books are often separated according to these and other classifications.

In making up a list, a publisher seeks diversity and balance, with fiction often the leading classification.

Within a trade publishing house, there are specialists in the acquisition and editing of various classifications. Some large publishers have separate imprints for particular trade classifications. For example, Macmillan's Howell Book House deals primarily with books on animals and pets. HarperCollins's imprint, Harper San Francisco, publishes only inspirational and religious books.

The Publisher's Backlist

Trade publishers issue new catalogs on a seasonal basis. These catalogs contain their new books and may also include their backlist books. Backlists are a publisher's books from previous seasons that continue to sell, and are reprinted as needed. Some publishers maintain a backlist ratio of five or ten times the number of current books.

Obviously, publishers promote their backlist because these are books whose editorial and production costs have already been paid for, and thus yield a handsome profit. One major trade publisher, Harcourt Brace Jovanovich, claims that its backlist accounts for 45 percent of the company's business.

When a publisher publishes a distinguished author, it will often maintain all of that author's previous works on its backlist. This not only strokes the author, but results in solid sales on a continuing basis. About half of all books at a bookstore are backlist books.

Category Nonfiction

Category nonfiction encompasses the group of trade books that deal with a specialized interest. All the books and products in this category are sold in bookstores and are available in libraries. There are also bookstores that specialize in individual categories such as cookbooks, mystery and crime, and New Age. We offer a description and background on a number of these categories.

Self-Improvement and Self-Help

Self-improvement and self-help books have been a mainstay of publishing for a long time. Recently, we have also seen a proliferation of books on codependence and recovery. One publisher, Health Press, has a list indicative of this trend. In 1992, it published *Suffer the Children: A Pediatrician's Reflection of Abuse, When You're Over the Hill You Begin to Pick Up Speed, Addiction: The High-Low Syndrome,* and *In Sickness and in Health: What Every Man Should Know About the*

Woman He Loves. Melody Beattie's *Codependent No More* sold more than three million copies.

How-To

One would think that every possible subject in how-to from how to build a Victorian gazebo to how to throw a slider has already been written, but not so. Recent entries in the how-to library have included *How to Succeed from a Support Position, How to Get into the Right Law School,* and *How to Get a Date with a Vampire (And What to Do with Him Once You've Got Him).*

Gardening and Home Improvement

Most large trade publishing houses publish books on gardening and home improvement. There are a number of publishers whose total output falls into this area. Sunset Publishing produces more than a dozen books a year on these subjects. There are more than two dozen others that publish exclusively in this category.

Cookbooks

The Fannie Farmer Cookbook is approaching its centenary; Knopf has recently published its thirteenth edition. The *Betty Crocker Cookbook* has sold more than twenty-six million copies. Craig Claiborne's *The New York Times Cook Book,* first published more than twenty years ago, has sold 2.5 million copies worldwide. Is there no limit to the public's appetite for books that tell you how to make and eat chocolate truffle tarts and lose weight at the same time? The answer is a resounding *no.*

Some large publishers put out a dozen or more cookbooks a year. Cookbook authors go on extensive publicity tours to promote their books. Most large cities have bookstores that sell cookbooks exclusively, and book superstores have large cookbook sections. The Book-of-the-Month Club has a HomeStyle Book Club. The classic work on vegetarian cooking, *The Moosewood Cookbook,* has sold more than one million copies, and there are dozens of others in this specialty.

Hundreds of new cookbooks are published each year, and no matter how exotic the title and subject matter, they continue to sell well.

My favorite titles are *White Trash Cooking* and *The Enchanted Broc-coli Forest.*

Business

Books on business have long been a staple of trade publishers. About fourteen hundred new business books are published yearly. Some large publishers maintain a separate imprint for their books on busi-ness subjects; others integrate them into their general list. There are also business book clubs. At this writing, two out of the top ten non-fiction best-sellers are business books.

Calendars

Each year, booksellers are offered an output of more than two hun-dred calendars produced by about a hundred different publishers. Large and small publishers participate in the "date" game. Random House publishes about twenty-five different calendars a year (includ-ing seven with the Sierra Club imprint). Although there are some high-priced calendars, most are priced in the $9.95 range, which seems to be a magic number in this category.

The subject matter of calendars covers a broad range of interests. One year, the eclectic mix included calendar subjects such as: Chinese Women Artists, Protect Our Planet, the Ultimate Sailing Calendar, Contemporary African Art, Cars Detroit Never Built, the EcoFreak Wall Calendar (365 wacky and wild ideas about saving the planet), and the class item, The Gorgeous Ladies of Wrestling.

New Age

New Age is a relatively new phenomenon. It encompasses the holis-tic view of body, mind, and spirit and includes Native American, Bud-dhist, and African traditions and philosophy in its subject matter. Although mainstream publishing houses publish New Age works, much of its output is produced by publishers who specialize in this field.

A listing for Timeless Books in a recent ABA Official Directory states that it publishes books on self-study, inspiration, and inner develop-ment, with such titles as *The Divine Light Invocation* and *Hatha Yoga:*

The Hidden Language. Many New Age books have sold in excess of a hundred thousand copies. One book, *The Celestine Prophecy*, has sold two million copies and is in print in 20 languages. There are specialized bookstores that sell only New Age.

Mystery and Murder

Mystery and its companion, murder, have long been a popular subject of trade book publishing. Hundreds of these books are published each year by mainstream and specialist publishers. As in other categories, there are bookstores dedicated to this special interest subject.

There is even a large group of women mystery writers headquartered in Raleigh, North Carolina, called Sisters in Crime. Its stated purpose is "To promote recognition of women's contribution to the field of mystery writing."

Vanity Presses and Self-Publishing

If you read *Writer's Digest* or the book review sections of large newspapers, you will see ads proclaiming "Publish it Yourself," or "Personal Publishing Gives Control/Profit to You." Self-publishing is a euphemism for what has been called "vanity presses." Basically, here's how it works. For an agreed fee from the author, a company will edit, proofread, typeset, design, and print a book. Some publishers also claim that they will handle sales to bookstores. Without vilifying these publishers as a group, we do urge caution in dealing with them.

Self-publishing can be accomplished effectively. Some self-published books have even made the best-seller list, but to be successful requires energy, know-how, and financing. An article in *The New York Times* discusses a success story in self-publishing.[1]

In 1992, Craig I. Zirbel self-published a book he wrote on his Kennedy assassination-conspiracy theory. The book took off and made the best-seller lists for many weeks. Of course, Zirbel had invested almost $100,000 and much time in the venture.

Most self-published books do not make it to the bookstores' shelves. Their authors inevitably use them as giveaways. If you choose to take this perilous approach to authordom, we recommend reading *The Complete Guide to Self-Publishing* by Tom and Marilyn Ross (Writer's Digest Books).

These fields of special interest show the diversity of trade book publishing. They also present fertile outlets for talented people with knowledge and background in particular areas.

Note

1. Esther B. Fein, "Some Self-Publishers Don't Perish," *The New York Times,* April 20, 1992, sec. D, p. 11.

Chapter 15

◆

Mass-Market and Trade Paperbacks

W e have established in the previous chapter the category of hardcover trade books. Now we will deal with paperbacks. There are two kinds of paperbacks: mass market and trade. Let's first look at mass market.

Mass-Market Paperbacks

In 1993, John Grisham's *A Time to Kill*, *The Pelican Brief*, and *The Firm* were the longest-running paperback best-sellers, accounting for many million-copy sales. Right behind Grisham in the ranking were Michael Crichton's *Jurassic Park, Rising Sun*, and *Congo*. Of course, the success of these books may be attributed to their exposure as movies, as well as hardcover editions.

Most mass-market paperback best-sellers, about 90 percent of the books that sold two million copies or more, are reprints of hardcover books. Each year about 120 paperbacks make the one-million-plus club. But not all these big-number megabooks make a profit for their publishers. We'll see why later in this chapter.

The mass-market paperback was created in 1939 by Robert deGraff, who then headed a new company called Pocket Books. World War II gave this hybrid a big boost once word got around that these light-weight, small-size books fit comfortably in the back pockets of GI uniforms. And, of course, they were inexpensive—about ten cents. Soon there were a number of publishers producing mass-market paperbacks of fiction and nonfiction trade books.

The Market Today

About twelve large publishers dominate the mass-market paperback field, issuing about ninety different titles a month. Another group of publishers contribute about three hundred additional paperback titles to this already crowded market. Popular fiction accounts for more than 75 percent of mass-market paperbacks published.

The highest-paid players in this league earn advances from half a million dollars on up per book.

Mass-market paperbacks are sold in bookstores, drugstores, college bookstores, supermarkets, convenience stores, and airline terminals. The books are distributed to about ninety thousand out-lets by a group of 450 independent wholesalers, who also distribute magazines.

The wholesalers ship books to the hundreds of outlets within their geographical territories. Problems arise because most nonbookstore outlets can only handle about fifteen or twenty titles, and this space is often reserved for best-sellers. Since most mass-market paperbacks are sold on a consignment basis, if the books don't sell fast, the covers are stripped and the books are returned to the wholesaler for full credit.

Let's look at the economics of mass-market paperbacks. Suppose that a publisher prints two hundred thousand copies of a $5.99 paperback. If 40 percent of the books are sold (the industry average), that's eighty thousand copies. The publisher's yield on each copy sold, after the wholesalers and national distributors take their cuts, is only about $2.40, multiplied by the eighty thousand sold copies, for a total of $192,000. From this, the publisher must pay an advance to the author, the cost of printing the books, and editorial and other in-house services. There surely is not much left for profit.

Publishers must therefore rely on getting their share of best-sellers, or publishing smaller quantities of books by authors who have established a niche, and are assured of selling a given number of copies of every book they write. In the field of science fiction, for example, about a dozen authors fit into this category. There are even special imprints for publishers in this genre.

Specialization is clearly a factor in mass-market publishing. There are "women's" authors like Danielle Steel, Jackie Collins, Belva Plain, Sidney Sheldon, and Judith Krantz. Then there are books by Stephen King, Ken Follett, Tom Clancy, and Joseph Wambaugh that predominantly appeal to men. Publishers also put out whole lines geared to special interests like westerns, adventure, romance, and mystery.

How Publishers Acquire Mass-Market Paperbacks

With lesser-known authors who write hardcover trade books, the originating publisher often holds the paperback rights and is free to sell these rights to anyone it chooses. The publisher may even retain the right for its own paperback imprint. More established authors retain paperback rights for themselves. If a hardcover trade book takes off, or if the author's works always sell well in paperback, there may be an auction for these rights.

If the hardcover publisher holds the rights, its subsidiary rights director and senior editor conduct the auction. If the author holds the rights, his or her agent runs the show. For paperback publishers, the publisher and senior acquisition editors participate in the bidding process.

When a paperback publisher buys a book for a large sum of money, it may do its own editing, and also institute its own promotion and publicity campaign.

The acquisition phase of mass-market paperbacks is often stressful but exciting at the same time. Jobs at a paperback publisher, however, are very much the same as they are at a hardcover trade house, with perhaps a bit less emphasis on the editorial side.

Trade Paperbacks

Fireside Trade Paperbacks is an imprint of Simon & Schuster. A recent catalog lists fifty-seven titles, none of which are fiction. Twenty-seven of these books are original, never having been published in hardcover. Trade paperbacks are printed on better paper than mass-market paperbacks, and as a result the average price for these books is $11 to $12, about midway between hardcover and mass-market paperbacks. The predominant size for these Fireside Books is 5 ¹/₂ by 8 ⁷/₁₆ inches. The subject matter of the books on this list mirrors that of Simon & Schuster's nonfiction hardcover line, with titles such as *Is Estrogen Right for You*, *7 Habits of Highly Effective People*, *Divorce Busting*, *Your Money, Your Self*, and *Baseball's Even Greater Insults*.

Recent best-selling trade paperbacks from other publishers include such titles as *Life's Little Instruction Book*, *The T-Factor Gram Counter*, *What to Expect When You're Expecting*, and Gloria Steinem's *Revolution From Within*.

Trade paperbacks have been with us for about forty years. They were formerly referred to as quality paperbacks, and in fact there is a major book club in this format, Quality Paperback Book Club, a sister to the Book-of-the-Month Club. The Quality Club has about a million members, and issues seventeen catalogs a year with twenty to twenty-five new books in each.

The earliest trade paperbacks were reprints of great literature, geared to the college market. Since their price was lower than the hardcover versions, trade paperbacks met with early success. Soon supplementary books for college courses were printed as trade paperbacks, sparking a minirevival movement in publishing circles. Today, the output of many university presses is in the trade paperback format. Trade paperbacks are also widely used by small, independent presses.

There are about a dozen major trade paperback imprints, primarily emanating from large hardcover publishers. Simon & Schuster has Fireside and Touchstone, Random House has Vintage, Doubleday has Anchor, and HarperCollins has HarperPerennial.

Although the number of trade paperbacks sold is only about 20 percent of mass-market paperbacks, it is estimated that they account for about 25 percent of all books sold in bookstores. One recent best-selling trade paperback was an original, *Life's Little Instruction Book,* which sold 3.39 million copies. About fifty trade paperbacks sell more than two hundred thousand copies a year.

Fiction is not a popular subject for best-selling trade paperbacks. Only one book, a reprint of Anne Rice's *The Witching Hour,* made the lists in recent years.

John Thornton, a veteran trade paperback editor, estimates that there are only a couple of hundred editors in the publishing industry who specifically work on trade paperbacks.[1] In determining where trade paperback editors get their ideas for books to publish, Thornton lists reprinting public-domain books, reprinting or simultaneous printing with in-house hardcovers, buying paperback reprints of hardcover books, and, finally, publishing a trade paperback of an original work.

Note

1. Gerald Gross, ed., *Editors on Editing* (New York: Harper & Row, 1985), 169.

Chapter 16

◆

The Making of a Best-Seller

Warner Books is an active participant in the book game, publishing a total of about three hundred books a year in both hardcover and paperback. In its roster are such best-selling novelists as Nelson DeMille, Carol Higgins Clark, Alexandra Ripley, and Ed McBain.

Warner Books' list now includes Robert James Waller. In 1993, novelist Waller set a best-selling record. His *Bridges of Madison County* was number one on the hardcover fiction list with more than 4.3 million copies sold, making it the best-selling novel of all time. In 1994, *Bridges* added 1.3 million in hardcover sales. By mid-1995 the book had been on the best-seller list for 145 weeks. Also in 1993, Waller's *Slow Waltz in Cedar Bend* sold almost two million copies. At one point, the author's two novels were number one and number two on the fiction hardcover best-seller list simultaneously. What is even more significant about Waller's achievement is that *Bridges* was a first novel.

In an interview in *American Bookseller,* Laurence Kirshbaum, head of Warner Books and Waller's publisher, told how Warner pulled off this noteworthy achievement.[1]

With *The Bridges of Madison County* Warner faced the challenge of a first novel by an unknown author. If the book was to succeed, it would need word of mouth among readers and booksellers to propel it above the mass of new novels published each year.

Warner also had a strong hunch that with careful promotion and marketing, *Bridges* could make it. It was a beautifully written love story and had appeal to both male and female readers. Warner took a gamble and sent five thousand free copies of the book to retailers, confident that if they saw it, felt it, read it, that they would get very excited about it.

The first printing for *Bridges* was twenty-nine thousand, a formidable number, yet far short of the press run Warner typically produced for one of its star authors. By comparison, after the success of *Bridges*, Warner had a first printing of 1.5 million for Waller's second novel, *Slow Waltz in Cedar Bend*.

The word of mouth for *Bridges* spread and its sales zoomed. "It was the right book at the right time," claimed Kirshbaum. "It was a book that touched the dreams and fantasies of millions of people in a very intimate and personal and meaningful way. It demonstrates the importance of not giving up on a book in the first couple of weeks. . . . Too often there is an expectation that if [a book] doesn't work in the first couple of weeks then it must be dead...get it into the back of the stores, send it back."

After the initial success, Warner kept promoting and publicizing the book, aided by the author's ubiquitous traveling around the country. The publisher continued sending the book out to prominent individuals in order to build up an inventory of positive quotes. It called hundreds of bookstores with encouraging news of big sales. Warner Books never decelerated its aggressive tactics, even after *Bridges* was an established success.

Warner's achievement with Waller's books is unique, particularly in an industry that publishes fifty thousand titles a year, and where less than 1 percent sell more than a hundred thousand copies. Ninety-nine percent sell imperceptible amounts, and even a best-selling book has revenues totaling less than 20 percent of a major movie.

Of course, the making of a best-seller by an established good-read author is considerably easier than Warner's efforts on behalf of

Robert James Waller's books. In 1990, Dell/Delacorte, a major publisher, signed Danielle Steel to a five-novel contract for an advance of *$60 million.* What may seem like madness is actually sound publishing economics. At the time Dell made the deal, Steel had more than 150 million copies of her books in print. In 1992, two of her books made the top ten hardcover best-seller lists. One of these books, *Jewels,* had a first printing of 1.2 million copies.

When a chain bookstore receives a new book from Steel, it is instantly placed at the entrance, usually in a twelve-copy floor display. It can't be missed. As a result of such exposure in the stores, in addition to television and print advertising campaigns, and the author's publicity efforts, the book rapidly rises to the top of the best-seller lists, thus enabling the chain to build more superstores, and the publisher to give multimillion-dollar advances to others in the charmed circle of best-selling authors of popular fiction.

Purists decry the diminished concern for the written word in best-selling fiction, proclaiming that once a tweedy haven for men and women of letters, publishing has become a noisy casino of chance, glamour, and high-risk investment.[2]

Respected literary agent Andrew Wylie adds that many titles on best-seller lists seem more like literary versions of prime-time television programs than original fiction. And, in fact, many of these novels are made into TV or theatrical movies. But we must face reality. Best-seller publishing is show business. These publishers make huge investments in their output and must retrieve a profit at the bookstore box office.

Hollywood purchases movie rights to novels by best-selling authors for huge sums for two basic reasons. First, these popular authors write books that often read like movies. But more important, when a book reaches best-seller status and becomes a movie, millions of potential moviegoers have already read the novel in hardcover or paperback.

Of course, buying movie rights to a novel doesn't always mean that the picture will be made. At any one point, the studios have a few dozen projects in development that never make it to the silver screen. Gay Talese's nonfiction book about our sex mores, *Thy Neighbor's Wife,* was optioned by United Artists in 1979 for the then-record sum of $2.5 million. The studio never made the movie.

Celebrities As Best-Selling Authors

The handful of best-selling popular fiction novelists can hardly fill the voracious appetites of publishers and their eager audiences. An alternative is publishing biographies and autobiographies of modern celebrities and living legends. In 1995, many of the top books in the nonfiction category were by or about such luminaries as Robert S. McNamara, Shirley MacLaine, Kathie Lee Gifford, Colin Powell, William J. Bennett, and Oprah Winfrey's cook, Rosie Daley.

Few celebrities write their own autobiographies, although some have insisted on doing so, usually to the chagrin of the publisher. One positive factor in publishing books about celebrities is their promotional value. A tour of the TV talk show circuit can reap rewards for these books beyond the limits of traditional authors.

What Drives Publishers in Their Quest for Best-Sellers

The world of best-sellerdom is peopled by a group of publishers whose principal motivation is the bottom line and their need to increase profits by at least 10 percent a year. Publishing efforts must be keyed to building authors in their stable and signing new ones who will achieve brand-name status, very much like a product in a supermarket.

Notes

1. Dan Cullen, "A Conversation with Laurence Kirshbaum," *American Bookseller* (November 1993): 37.

2. Josh Getlin, "Warning: Danger Ahead," *Los Angeles Times*, May 22, 1992, sec. E, p. 1.

Chapter 17

◆

The Children's Book Success Story

A visitor to the medieval city of Bologna, Italy, in April may gorge on such gastronomic gems as tortellini, tortelloni, and tagliatelle in a restaurant housed in a thirteenth-century tower; visit one of Europe's oldest universities; and if the visitor is there on children's book business, review the many-colored wares of fourteen hundred publishers from sixty countries at the Bologna Children's Book Fair, the industry's premier showcase.

The Bologna Children's Book Fair is where rights to books are bought and sold, and also a place for illustrators to discuss their work with others and to show their portfolios to publishers from many nations.

So international in scope is the field of children's books that at a recent Bologna Children's Book Fair there were thirteen publishers from China, fourteen from South Africa, and eight from Ghana, in addition to hundreds from Europe and North America.

The Scope of Children's Books Today

In the book business they are officially called "juveniles," although most professionals still refer to them as children's books. Whatever the name, children's books are one of the book industry's giant success stories. We offer some staggering statistics, but first, a definition of the category. Juvenile trade books cover a broad range from picture books for toddlers to stories and themes for young adults in their late teens.

Now for the numbers. Of the approximately fifty thousand books published each year, about five thousand, or just over 10 percent, are children's books. In net sales at retail, their total is more than $1 *billion*, or double their dollar volume in 1986. At a recent American Booksellers Association book convention, about five hundred publishers displayed a children's book line.

At this writing, there are about five hundred children's bookstores across the nation. The large Barnes & Noble and Borders-Walden chains now have bookstores exclusively for children, and their superstores have children's book sections containing hundreds of different titles.

Since the early 1990s the Doubleday Book Club and the Book-of-the-Month Club have included children's book clubs. They operate like traditional book clubs, and typically give discounts on their offerings.

The major book wholesalers and distributors are significantly involved in this field. One large distributor, Ingram, carries about twenty thousand different children's book titles in its inventory.

What Is a Children's Book Best-Seller?

In 1991, the adored Dr. Seuss (Theodore Geisel) died. That year, *Six by Seuss* sold 297,750 copies at a $25 price. For 1992, ten of his backlist titles (books of previous seasons that are still in print) had combined sales of more than 2.35 million copies.

In one recent year, thirty children's books sold a hundred thousand copies or more in hardcover, one hundred paperbacks sold a hundred thousand copies or more, and the perennial favorite *Aladdin* sold more than one million copies in hardcover. Small wonder that children's book acquisition editors receive so many submissions.

The Children's Book Acquisition Process

An article in *Publishers Weekly* delineates the plight of the acquisitions editors at children's book publishers, and the slim odds of breaking into this field as an illustrator or writer. [1]

It has been estimated that the acceptance rate for children's book submissions is one-fourth of 1 percent, or four acceptances in a thousand submissions. How then does this highly selective process work? Most large children's book publishers have departments staffed by several editors, each with a degree of specialization. As in the other areas of trade publishing, raw unsolicited submissions, otherwise known as "slush," are handled by editorial assistants and assistant editors. In addition, the slush team has an assistant art director or assistant design editor. At many houses, the slush pile is so profuse that freelance readers are hired to evaluate submissions and submit reports on their findings.

The task of reading submissions has become so taxing and expensive that many children's book publishers no longer accept unsolicited manuscripts, a policy many have adopted for all their books. These publishers often prefer that the writer or illustrator send a written query first describing the project. If the query sounds promising to an editor, the writer may be asked to come in to discuss the proposal.

What do children's book editors look for in a submission? Of course, the obvious answer is another Maurice Sendak or Dr. Seuss, but realistically, one editor defines her quest as, "an original voice or a strong character." Another editor says that she looks for writing that creates an emotional response. Look at a dozen children's books and you'll find these qualities quite evident.

In terms of art, the preferred approach for editors is to look at as many portfolios as possible in order to find the visual qualities and excitement necessary to make a children's book stand out. A number of children's book publishers schedule regular meetings to evaluate new artists' portfolios.

One successful children's illustrator, Tom Pohrt, answers the question about what you need to break into children's illustration:

> *Have a portfolio that shows a consistent vision, so that an editor can see what direction you've taken and match you up with the right writer. The work is everything. I don't think it's a case where the more people you meet, the better off you are. I just walked into Farrar, Straus and six months later got a call to illustrate Miko. That says to me it's a wide-open field.*
>
> *Being self-taught means a lot of stumbling around. I took an art course in college and all but flunked out.[2]*

Getting an agent is still the soundest approach to breaking into children's book writing and illustration. Agents receive about 15 percent commission for their services. Check *Literary Market Place* in your library. Under agents, it lists about fifty agents with children's books as their specialty. Later in this chapter we discuss the Children's Book Council and the Society of Children's Book Writers and Illustrators. These groups may be helpful in locating a reputable agent.

Once you become one of the fortunate few who get published, you won't become rich unless you're Maurice Sendak, Dr. Seuss, the Berenstains, or Martin Handford of *Waldo* fame. The advances in children's book publishing are slim, running about $1,000 each for artist and writer, against a total royalty of 10 percent.

CAREER TIP

If you are determined to make it as a creator of children's books, the Children's Book Council offers four valuable pamphlets to guide your search:

◆ *Children's Book Council Members List.* Includes the names of publishing house members, addresses, key personnel, description of types of books published, and size of list ($1 plus 64¢ postage).

◆ *Illustrator's Guide to Members of the Children's Book Council.* Names and addresses of personnel in member publishing houses who are responsible for reviewing portfolios; includes guidelines for submitting work ($3 plus 64¢ postage).

◆ *Writing Children's Books.* Pamphlet for writers about children's book publishing ($2 plus 32¢ postage).

◆ *Illustrating Children's Books.* Pamphlet for illustrators about children's book publishing ($2 plus 32¢ postage).

To receive these pamphlets, send a 6-by-9-inch stamped, self-addressed envelope to Children's Book Council, 568 Broadway, Suite 404, New York, NY 10012.

Women in Children's Book Publishing

A recent members list of the Children's Book Council shows thirty-seven publishers that publish fifty or more books a year. Of this group, thirty-two are run by women, with such titles as editorial director, publisher, and editor-in-chief. Although salaries at the entry level in this field are low, women at the top rung in children's book publishing earn from $50,000 to well over $100,000 a year.

Women are employed at every level of children's book publishing: as acquisition editors, editors, art directors and designers, sales and marketing people, production managers, assistant editors, and editorial assistants.

The Society of Children's Book Writers and Illustrators

The Society of Children's Book Writers and Illustrators (SCBWI), founded in 1968, is an excellent professional organization for writers and illustrators of children's literature. Its primary purpose is to act as a network for the exchange of knowledge between writers, illustrators, editors, publishers, agents, librarians, educators, bookstore personnel, and others involved with literature for young people.

SCBWI issues a bimonthly publication to its members, and sponsors a free manuscript and illustration exchange among its members. It also conducts periodic meetings and workshops in key regions of the country. Once a year, SCBWI sponsors a national conference with lectures, workshops, and individual manuscript and art consultation.

To inquire about the many benefits of this organization, write to Society of Children's Book Writers and Illustrators, P.O. Box 66296, Mar Vista Station, Los Angeles, CA 90066.

If your interest lies in children's books, as an editor, writer, or illustrator, read *Publishers Weekly* for excellent coverage on this specialization. In your job search, focus first on the big guys. One publisher, Bantam, Doubleday, Dell Books for Your Readers, has nineteen separate imprints, or lines. In total they publish more than four hundred books a year.

And, of course, read children's books to see what makes them stand out.

Notes

1. Shannon Maughan, "Panning for Gold," *Publishers Weekly* (May 3, 1991): 42.

2. "Editor's Choice," *American Bookseller* (August 1990): 136.

Chapter 18

◆

Small Presses:
Eclectic in Outlook

J oseph Simon runs his publishing enterprise from his house on the crest of a hill in Malibu overlooking the beach and the blue-green Pacific Ocean. Simon's Pangloss Press, named after Voltaire's optimistic character in *Candide*, is categorized as a "small press," one of about five thousand small presses throughout the United States. Every year Simon publishes one or two new books, each taste-fully designed and printed on recycled or acid-free paper. His cata-log lists a backlist of about twenty books, primarily on the subject of Judaica.

Small presses publish books on subjects the big publishers veer away from such as poetry, art, architecture, local history, mysticism, and alternative religions. Small press runs range from one thousand to four thousand copies, and few release more than four or five books a season. That's why they're called small presses.

Because they're small, these publishers cannot afford advances beyond $1,000 to $2,000. Yet authors seek out small presses when their works are not considered commercial enough for the major publishers, and also because authors know the small press will sup-port a book in a manner not always possible at big houses.

Although many small presses do not choose to go public about it, they do accept unsolicited manuscripts. This does not mean, however, that a poorly written work will have a better chance of being published by a small press. On the contrary, the standards of small presses may be higher than those of the large houses. Nevertheless, knowing that their works will at least be considered provides encouragement to many authors.

At a small press each book purchased is a significant investment. The author is treated with great respect. The creation itself is the foremost priority. The small-press editor displays a high degree of optimism, a trait not always shared by his or her major-publisher counterparts. The author feels the total experience of participating in an effort that is harmonious, confident, creative, and inspiring.

The Diversified Output of Small Presses

The output of small presses, sometimes called "independent presses," is indeed diversified. A recent issue of American Bookseller ran a feature titled "Highlights of the New Season from Independent Presses." Here are a few selections from that list:

> The Island of Floating Women, published by Clothespin Fever Press, San Diego.
>
> The Dada Almanac, published by High Risk Press Books, New York.
>
> ZAP: How Your Computer Can Hurt You and What You Can Do About It, published by Peachpit Press, Berkeley, California.
>
> Writing Across Cultures: A Handbook on Writing Poetry and Lyrical Prose, published by Blue Heron Publishing, Hillsboro, Oregon.
>
> John Rosemond's Daily Guide to Parenting, published by Thoughtful Books, Marshalltown, Iowa.

The same issue reviews ten books of poetry, definitely high-risk for larger publishers.

Focus on Four Walls Eight Windows

When a senior editor at a large publishing house is asked to name the best small press, the odds favor he or she will choose Four Walls Eight Windows. Four Walls was formed in New York in 1987 by John Oakes and Dan Simon, two young publishing professionals with a determination to publish the kind of literary works not considered commercial enough for the large publishing houses.

By the end of 1994, Four Walls had published eighty titles, including Michael Brodsky's highly regarded avant-garde novel *X-Man*; the provocative work *A Woman's Book of Choices: Abortion, Menstrual Extraction, RU-486*; an important book on the continuing "war" with Japan, *Japanese Rage: Japanese Business and its Assault on the West*; three of Nelson Algren's fiction masterpieces, *The Man with the Golden Arm*, *The Neon Wilderness*, and *Never Come Morning*; and comic strip artist Harvey Pekar and Joyce Brabner's *Our Cancer Year*.

For its spring 1995 list, Four Walls Eight Windows published only eleven titles—four fiction, one on bicycles, one of Samuel Beckett's plays, a war correspondent's memoir of Vietnam and Cambodia, a book on nutrition, an exposé of the news that wasn't covered by the media, a look backward in science fiction, and the selected short stories of Sherwood Anderson.

Four Walls pays royalties and cash advances on all its books. For a first novel it pays at least $1,000. For a strong work of nonfiction it pays in the $3,000 to $5,000 range. To reduce overhead, this publisher farms out publicity, copyediting, and design. It does not have an in-house sales staff, relying instead on Publishers Group West, the nation's largest independent distributor, which represents about 180 small independent publishers. Publishers Group West is important enough to have multiple booths at the American Booksellers Association convention, with twenty-five of its staffers on hand.

For foreign rights sales, Four Walls is represented by Writers House, which has subagents around the world. Four Walls sells other rights in-house, and in its short publishing history has already sold a number of paperback rights, and a couple of movie options.

Having started with an investment of under $100,000, Four Walls Eight Windows is clearly a success story in the world of small presses. Should others try it? Maybe, but only if they have the experience and financing. By the way, how did Four Walls Eight Windows arrive at its offbeat name? Says Oakes, "We didn't want to sound like a law firm . . . we didn't want to sound like anything."

Life on the Lonely Planet

Would you like to travel to exotic Mongolia, Outback Australia, Afghanistan, and Sri Lanka, write about these places and then publish the books yourself? That's what Tony and Maureen Wheeler, founders of Lonely Planet Publications, have been doing successfully since 1973. Their first book, *Across China on the Cheap*, was hand-stapled and hand-sold. It sold out in about ten days. Says Maureen Wheeler: "We didn't see it as a business; we saw it as a way to finance our travel."[1]

After taking the slow boat to China and making a profit on it, the Wheelers began to turn their travel addiction into a successful publishing operation. The formula was simple: Do books on places you want to go.

At this writing, Lonely Planet has more than one hundred titles in print and a staff of about fifty people. The Wheelers still travel on research for new books. Their newest entry: a *Europe on a Shoestring* series.

C A R E E R   T I P

Readers who are capable of writing quality literary fiction and poetry should consider submitting their work to a small press. The chances of being published are slim, as are the advances if one is accepted; yet the reward of being published by a high-quality small press is to be accepted in the inner circle of literature.

Would-be authors would be well advised to check publishers' listings in the *Literary Market Place* so that they don't send a highly specific type of proposal to a house that doesn't publish that type of material. Small presses are major users of freelance specialists, particularly editors.

Smaller Publishers Play on the World Stage

An article in *Publishers Weekly* discusses the success of small presses in selling their works for foreign publication.[2]

One publisher, Avery Publishing Group of Garden City, New York, has sold five of its titles to overseas publishers. Its *Sharks Don't Get Cancer* sold to ten countries in fifteen language versions; its *Love Tactics* made nine sales, and *Macrobiotic Way* seven sales.

Impact Publishers of San Luis Obispo, California, sold its self-development book *Liking Myself* to a small Japanese publisher. That publisher sold more than 150,000 copies and used it as a bilingual school reader.

Conference of Small Magazine/Press Editors and Publishers (COSMEP)

In 1968, a small number of small publishers met at Berkeley to form a support group. They called themselves the Conference of Small Magazine/Press Editors and Publishers. Later the name was shortened to COSMEP. Its purpose was to provide common action for its membership, and to improve distribution and marketing efforts.

Today, COSMEP has fifteen hundred members in the United States and twelve foreign countries. Its services include a monthly newsletter, a co-op advertising program, and combined trade exhibits at the American Booksellers Association convention, American Library

Association convention, and the Frankfurt Book Fair. COSMEP also provides support services to its membership including a credit information service, professional seminars and conferences, insurance, and discounts on office supplies.

If you are interested in forming a small press, by all means join COSMEP. Its annual membership fee is only $60. Write to COSMEP, P.O. Box 420703, San Francisco, CA 94142-0703; (415) 922-9490.

If you are thinking of starting a small press, you should understand that most of these operations don't make money. Before embarking on one of these precarious enterprises, one needs experience, creativity, and, the most important ingredient, adequate financing.

Working for a small press can also be worthwhile and rewarding. At such a press, you won't be pigeonholed into one department with no sense of what's happening on the next floor, as might be the case when working for a large publisher. Because most have small staffs, you have the opportunity of assuming two, three, or more job functions. The salary may be less, but what better way to learn the craft of book publishing?

Notes

1. Gaye Quaranta, "Across Asia and Into Business," *American Bookseller* (January 1993): 80.

2. John F. Baker, "Smaller Publishers Play on World Stage," *Publishers Weekly* (November 28, 1994): 34.

Chapter 19

———————— ◆ ————————

The Scholarly World of University Presses

An ad for the Columbia University Press in the 1995 ABA Official Directory lists twenty new books of diverse interest including:

The Columbia Anthology of British Poetry

The FDR Years: On Roosevelt and His Legacy

Floods of Fortune: Ecology and Economy Along the Amazon

Romantic Passion: A Universal Experience

From Peep Show to Palace: The Birth of American Film

Adcult USA: The Triumph of Advertising in American Culture

Invented Moralities: Sexual Values in an Age of Uncertainty

Journeys in Microspace: Images from a Scanning Electron Microscope

The books in this ad represent only a portion of Columbia's yearly output—about 150 new books in total on dozens of subjects, academic and general.

Columbia is one of the oldest and largest university presses in the United States. Founded in 1893, it today maintains a backlist of more than three thousand titles.

Johns Hopkins University is the oldest American university press, dating from 1878. It, too, conducts an active publishing program with about 160 new titles a year. It has a staff of thirty-five, including a half-dozen who work in acquisitions. One recent Johns Hopkins release, *The Thirty-six Hour Day,* a book about Alzheimer's Disease, sold 250,000 copies in hardcover and the same number in paperback.

There are approximately 120 university presses in the United States. They publish about eight thousand titles a year and account for about $325 million in publishers' net book sales, less than 2 percent of all books.

Typically, the production of university presses is directed toward the publication of scholarly works of nonfiction. Although there is some favorable consideration given to a university's own faculty, most presses maintain high standards of objectivity in their selection process.

Many books emanating from university presses are geared to academics in specific disciplines at other universities; however, there are some titles with appeal to students and the general public, and occasionally even fiction appears on their lists.

Because print quantities of these books are small, the advances received by their authors are small as well. Of course, in the "publish or perish" atmosphere of academia, authors do not write these books for financial considerations.

For the most part, university presses are not-for-profit organizations, and don't publish to make money. Their principal customers are scholars and libraries, with college bookstores absorbing some of their sales. However, in recent years, university presses have pursued the trade market through sales in general bookstores. Since maintaining a sales force is quite costly, university presses often join consortia that sell to the trade on behalf of a number of presses.

The Association of American University Presses

The Association of American University Presses (AAUP) is a one-hundred-member organization founded in 1937. Its membership embraces small university presses that produce only a handful of titles, as well as those publishing hundreds each year. AAUP's activities cover copyright, education and training, marketing, and library relations.

There are subcommittees of AAUP dealing with such subjects as bias-free language, government and foundation relations, and equal opportunity.

CAREER TIP

While you're still in college or graduate school, try for an internship at your college's press, even if the job is unpaid. You'll gain valuable experience that will certainly help when you look for a job after graduation.

Submitting Manuscripts to University Presses

AAUP's directory has a valuable section on how to submit manuscripts to university presses. Here are some highlights:

- Research the best university press for your book.

- Take advantage of presses' past experience in certain subjects.

- Read university presses' advertisements in journals in your field.

- Call the appropriate acquisition editor for an appointment.

- Prepare a manuscript prospectus based on standards established by university presses and the AAUP. See its annual directory for these guidelines.

For information on AAUP's directory, newsletter, and other publications write to: Publications Department, Association of American University Presses, Inc., 584 Broadway, Suite 410, New York, NY 10012.

Chapter 20

◆

Religious, Inspirational, Bible, and New Age Books

In 1989, Gold 'n' Honey Books, an imprint of Questar Publishers, located in the tiny town of Sisters, Oregon, published the *Beginner's Bible,* a 528-page children's bible. At the time of this writing, the *Beginner's Bible* is in its third year as the best-selling Christian children's book and has sold 1.7 million copies.

Joseph F. Girzone retired from the active priesthood in 1986 for health-related reasons. He had never written before when he began a fulfilling career as a novelist of three best-selling works featuring Joshua, the pious woodcarver.

Clearly, there is a renaissance of spirituality in the 1990s and, concomitantly, in what is called religious publishing. Some regard this quest as a counterbalance to the turbulence of our society, while others see it as a radical return to spiritual values. Whatever the compelling motivation, the result is clear—sales of religious books have had an upsurge in recent years.

The Wide Scope of Religious Books

The religious book category has come to include not only bibles and traditional books of faith, but also inspirational, New Age, and works of mysticism. So, for example, in a conventional bookstore, we might see *The Essential Jesus* alongside *The Book of Blessings: A Recreation of Jewish Prayer,* Shambhala's *Living in the New Consciousness*, a book dealing with Zen by a Jesuit priest, and the contemporary work of renewed Christianity, *The Coming of the Cosmic Christ.*

There are more than three thousand new books published in this field each year. The total annual sales volume for the category exceeds $900 million. A recent edition of *Literary Market Place* lists eighty publishers whose output is predominantly books on Catholicism, more than one hundred that focus on Protestantism, about forty on Judaism, and 125 that are in the religious other category.

At the 1994 ABA Convention, almost two hundred publishers represented published books in the New Age category. Many publish exclusively in this category. In addition to books, they also produce audio and video discourse tapes, meditation sequences, and music. A trade association, New Age Publishing and Retailing Alliance (NAPRA) serves book retailers, publishers, authors, and editors in this burgeoning field.

In terms of bookstores, 70 percent of general bookstores carry religious books, with an average of 250 titles in each store. There are also thousands of religious bookstores across the nation. The Christian Booksellers Association has thirty-five member stores. The Mountain and New England regions have the highest sales activity in religious books, while the South Atlantic region has the lowest sales average.

Bibles account for 25 percent of the sales of religious books, inspirational represents 18 percent, motivational/self-help 17 percent, and children's religious books 11 percent.

One large mainstream publisher, HarperCollins, is a major participant in religious book publishing. A recent religious best-sellers list appearing in *Publishers Weekly* had two titles issued on the

HarperCollins imprint, *Tao Te Ching* and *The Gospel According to Jesus*, and another book, *The Historical Jesus*, published under its Harper San Francisco division.

A recent advertisement for Harper San Francisco in *Publishers Weekly* is indicative of the range of titles of a religious imprint. It included *Born of a Woman; Roget's Thesaurus of the Bible; Holy Siege: The Year That Shook Catholic America; Prayer: Finding the Heart's True Home; The Gospel of Thomas*; and *Mother Teresa*.

Zondervan is a wholly owned subsidiary of HarperCollins. It describes itself as "the leading international Christian communications company." This specialized publisher employs fifteen hundred people nationwide and publishes about 130 titles a year.

Word, another major religious publisher, headquartered in Dallas, had two titles on a recent religious best-sellers list. They included the Rev. Pat Robertson's *The New World Order*, which made the list for many weeks, and Barbara Johnson's *Stick a Geranium in Your Hat and Be Happy*. Billy Graham is another Word author.

Publishers Weekly also publishes a Christian best-sellers list. On a recent listing, in addition to titles from Zondervan and Word, other religious publishers such as Bethany House, Thomas Nelson, and Crossway Books were well represented.

Alfred A. Knopf's *The Prophet*, by Kahlil Gibran, a perennial religious best-seller, has been in continuous publication since 1938.

Some religious authors, such as Word's Rev. Charles Swindoll, have achieved mass audience popularity. His recent best-sellers include *Growing Deep in the Christian Faith* and *Simple Faith*. Swindoll, who has written twenty-two books as of this writing, is among the nation's top-selling authors in all categories.

In 1992, one enterprising religious publisher, Gospel Light/Regal Books, formed a consortium with publishers in the former Soviet Union to publish, print, and distribute religious books. Its initial output included ten books for adults and several children's books. Religious publishing has spread its wings all over the world. A children's Bible story series from publisher Arch Books has even been translated into Chinese and Vietnamese.

151

Careers in Religious Publishing

Most jobs in this field are similar to those in mainstream publishing. However, religion majors have the edge in the editorial phase of this specialty. Consult *Literary Market Place* for a listing of religious publishers. Another positive factor for job-seekers is that religious publishers are located all over the country.

Chapter 21

♦

The Educational Scene

Today, artificial intelligence is no longer a remote concept relegated to the science fiction novel. Yet, the reality of a "thinking" computer was first delineated almost fifty years ago in Norbert Weiner's groundbreaking work *Cybernetics*, published by a distinguished publisher in this field, John Wiley & Sons.

Wiley is one of the most prominent names in professional publishing. Founded in 1807 by Charles Wiley as a small printing plant in downtown New York City, the tiny company later branched out to become a bookstore and publishing operation. Its early output included law books, language texts, and a new genre—the American novel.

By 1915, Wiley became recognized for publishing the best in scientific literature. In the years before World War II, the company widened its sphere to include business and professional books. I can remember studying two Wiley books, *Principles of Radio* and *Elements of Electricity*, both having sold in the hundreds of thousands.

In the 1950s, worldwide interest in science escalated with the Soviet Union's launching of *Sputnik*. Wiley became an international scientific publisher with the publication of the nuclear scientists Edward Teller, Harold Urey, and Hans Bethe.

Here are some landmark books published by Wiley, which give an indication of the range of this company:

- ◆ *Physics,* by David Halliday and Robert Resnick. This popular book uses easy, almost colloquial, language and cartoons ("Peanuts" is a favorite) to explain technical concepts.

- ◆ *General Virology,* by S. E. Luria (Nobel Prize winner).

- ◆ *The Rorschach: A Comprehensive System,* by John E. Exner, Jr. This work sets forth the first cohesive system for scoring and interpreting the Rorschach projective psychological test.

- ◆ *Basic Inorganic Chemistry,* by Geoffrey Wilkinson (Nobel Prize winner).

- ◆ *Cybernetics,* by Norbert Weiner.

Four recent Wiley Professional catalogs were separated into Earth Sciences and the Environment; Life Sciences, Medical Sciences and Related Areas; Chemistry and Related Areas; and Mathematics, Statistics, Physics and Optics and Optical Engineering.

The books in these catalogs are published in paperback and cloth (hardbound), and are priced from as low as $12.95 to $1,360 for a six-volume set of the *Handbook of Applicable Mathematics.*

John Wiley & Sons publishes about fifteen hundred books and related information products each year and maintains a backlist of about nine thousand titles in four hundred disciplines. It has a roster of approximately eleven thousand authors and thirteen hundred employees worldwide. Incidentally, Wiley's headquarters is still in New York. The company has annual net sales of more than $200 million.

The category of professional book publishing encompasses a broad range of disciplines and professions. It includes textbooks in the fields of law, medicine, business, science, mathematics, computers, and books for working professionals in these areas.

Each year there are about fourteen hundred books published on business, twelve hundred on law, twenty-seven hundred on science, and more than three thousand on medicine in the broad scope of professional book publishing. *Literary Market Place (LMP)* lists approximately five hundred publishers in the scientific and technical categories alone.

C A R E E R   T I P

Publishers in this field are located all across the country. If you think your talents qualify you for employment with these companies, consult for names and addresses.

The Computer Book Publishing Revolution

They say that Bill Gates, the young guiding genius behind Microsoft, is almost as wealthy as the Sultan of Brunei. Gates gained his fortune with Microsoft, the company that created the hugely successful Word and Windows computer software packages.

Making effective and creative use of these programs has given rise to a miniflood of computer books in recent years. There are more than 250 books on WordPerfect alone. One book distributor claims that in a recent two-month period he had been offered forty books on DOS-5. Yet each announcement of new computer books brings a torrent of titles that inundate an already overblown market.

In spring 1992, when Microsoft released its Windows 3.1 operating system, it had by then sold more than nine million copies of the original Windows. To guide purchasers on the use of Windows 3.1, more than a dozen publishers issued books on it in only the first three months of its introduction. Leading the publishing pack, Microsoft itself published ten books on this new software.

For the buyers of these computer books, information on a new system does not come cheap. Microsoft's *Windows 3.1 Programmer's Reference Library* of six volumes costs $180. There are, however, valid reasons for these high prices. From the publisher's standpoint, the books are expensive to produce, requiring an elaborate editing process and high-priced authors.

Computer publishing's output consists of books, book/disc combinations, guides, tutorials, and reference manuals for PC novices, programmers, and just plain dabblers. Periodically, *Publishers Weekly* publishes its list of computer best-sellers, which is broken out into the leaders on operating systems, applications, general, and Macintosh. In July 1995, the "dummy" concept dominated the list. IDG, a large publishing organization in this field, had the following hot dummy winners:

Operating Systems

No. 1   *Windows 3.11 for Dummies, 3rd ed.*

No. 2   *DOS for Dummies, 2nd ed.*

No. 3   *Windows 95 for Dummies*

No. 6   *More Windows 3.1 for Dummies*

No. 7   *More DOS for Dummies*

Applications

No. 1   *Word 6 for Windows for Dummies*

No. 2   *WordPerfect 6.1 for Windows for Dummies*

No. 3   *Excel for Dummies, 2nd ed.*

No. 6   *Access for Dummies*

No. 7   *1-2-3 for Dummies, 2nd ed.*

General

No. 2   *Internet for Dummies*

No. 3   *PCs for Dummies*

Macintosh

No. 1   *Macs for Dummies*

No. 3   *More Macs for Dummies*

No. 6   *Clarisworks 3.0 for Macs for Dummies*

Conclusion: It makes good publishing sense to appeal to computer dummies, although *The Complete Idiot's Guide to DOS 6* and *Macs for Morons* did not make the list.

CAREER TIP

There are about fifty publishers that publish a half-dozen or more computer books each year. Consider computer publishing as a career choice, especially if your training and background is oriented in this direction. Editorial salaries are higher than in general trade publishing, particularly at the entry level. Publishers are decentralized, which is significant for those who don't choose to work in New York City. Read *Publishers Weekly* for its twice-a-year major coverage of computer publishing. At your library consult *Books in Print* and, under "Computer Books," jot down the names of the publishers that publish these books. Then research these publishers in *Literary Market Place* for names, addresses, and other salient information about the companies.

Textbooks and Reference Books

Forty years ago, the choice of textbooks to be used in the classroom was made at the statewide level. Once a book was adopted, it was used for as many as five to seven years. Today, publishers of textbooks must be concerned with considerations of content including ethnic and racial mix, and readability formulas, such as the number of multisyllabic words in a sentence. There are focus groups to do evaluations, and most important, high-tech systems of teacher's aids, including guides, videos, disks, and other sophisticated material.

Today's elementary and high school textbook is adopted in a lengthy and rigid process by a state, city, or local school district or board of education, working closely with school superintendents and special textbook committees consisting of administrators and teachers.

The Scope of Textbook Publishing Today

There are more than thirty million students nationwide in kindergarten through eighth grade in both public and private schools. The dollar volume for the sales of all elementary and high school texts (elhi) is about $2 billion a year.

Educational publishing is the largest and, without question, the most profitable segment of publishing, with profit margins of 20 percent or more.

Many book publishers vie for this large and lucrative market. There are about a hundred elementary and 130 high school textbook publishers listed in *LMP*. These publishers overlap, since many produce both elementary and high school texts, and some publish college texts as well.

Focus on Silver Burdett Ginn

Silver Burdett Ginn, a division of Simon & Schuster, one of the world's largest publishing organizations, is itself the industry's foremost elhi publisher. Ginn started as a reading-text publisher in 1867, while Silver Burdett, which specialized in mathematics and science textbooks, originated in 1885. The two companies merged in 1986.

The combined company produces textbooks and related materials that supplement basic texts, such as interactive video products, multicultural resources, films, and workbooks. A recent series, *The World of Reading*, developed by Silver Burdett Ginn, is estimated to have cost $40 million. In its preparation, the company used two thousand children in a series of focus groups. It is estimated that fully half of the nation's thirty million kindergarten through eighth grade students read Silver Burdett Ginn books. Its entire line encompasses about nine thousand books in print.

To attract the schools to its diversified line, Silver Burdett Ginn has one of the largest sales forces in the industry, about a hundred people, many of them former teachers. In addition to the domestic market, Silver Burdett Ginn sells its books and other educational products to more than a hundred foreign countries.

College Textbooks

More than three hundred publishers compete in the lush college textbooks market. Some issue hundreds of new titles each year and maintain backlists of ten times that number. Included in this mix are texts about such diverse disciplines as anthropology, theater, computer science, educational psychology, and mass communications.

The very nature of the college textbook has changed dramatically in recent years. Industry analyst John Dessauer points out that today's college textbook is part of a text "package," which includes a core book, tests, solution manuals, study guides, workbooks, and teaching aids for the instructor. Dessauer also notes that a successful text package in a basic subject can have an annual volume of a hundred thousand copies.[1]

Technology has also made a difference in the preparation of material for the college market. A publisher can deliver the "textbook" in print, as well as on-line, on CD-ROM, on film, and on interactive laser disks. One publisher uses a new system known as electronic manuscript management (EMM) to make users comfortable with the new technology. Of course, new technology demands retraining for editors and writers, and invites the participation of new people familiar with this environment.

An advantage, too, for job seekers in the whole field of educational publishing is the diversified location of publishers across the country. There are, for example, major publishers in Belmont, California; Carthage and Deerfield, Illinois; Minneapolis, Minnesota; Englewood Cliffs and Old Tappan, New Jersey; and Cleveland and Columbus, Ohio. In applying for internships and jobs in this field, consult the *LMP*.

As of this writing, in terms of size, the ranking of the largest U.S. educational publishers is as follows:

1. Simon & Schuster Educational Publishing

2. Harcourt Brace Jovanovich

3. Scholastic Inc.

4. Houghton Mifflin Company

5. McGraw-Hill/Macmillan Book Company

Dictionaries and Reference Books

One of the reference works I use is *The Random House Dictionary of the English Language*, Second Edition, Unabridged. It has 315,000 entries in twenty-five hundred pages and includes fifty thousand new words and seventy-five thousand new meanings from the previous edition, which was copyrighted in 1983. This indispensable bulk of knowledge and information weighs eleven pounds. One cannot possibly author any book without this or a comparable dictionary.

The staff of *The Random House Dictionary* is considerable, with an editor-in-chief and managing editor at the top, ten senior editors, an assistant managing editor, five editors, three pronunciation editors, and five assistant editors. At the support level, the staff includes ten editorial assistants, ten proofreaders, four copy editors, research assistants, etymology assistants, artists, and production and design people.

Key to the preparation of a work such as *The Random House Dictionary* is its group of consultants on individual subjects. It lists about three hundred consultants and another fifty special consultants.

Although *The Random House Dictionary* is a single-volume work, many other reference books are multivolume; for example, the *Encyclopedia Britannica*. Reference books represent a huge investment in research and must be constantly revised. Some are issued annually; others even more frequently.

Many reference books, particularly encyclopedias, are sold by direct sales or direct mail. About 90 percent of these books are marketed to individuals, with the balance sold to schools and public libraries.

In the business field, reference books are traditionally sold by subscription. An advertising agency, for example, uses dozens of different reference books, some that are published monthly.

Textbook and reference book publishing is hardly a glamorous area. It does, however, offer job stability. The marketing phase of this field is both sophisticated and challenging.

Note

1. John P. Dessauer, *Book Publishing: What It Is, What It Does* (New York: R. R. Bowker Co., 1981), 67.

Part IV

How Books Are Sold

Chapter 22

---◆---

How Publishers Handle Domestic and International Sales

A t the tiny Big and Tall (not a clothing store), a superhip bookshop in Los Angeles that is open on weekends until 4 A.M., you can sip cappuccino while browsing through a book on the philosophy of Nietzsche. Among Manhattan's Upper West Side attractions is a block-long Barnes & Noble superstore that offers a choice of 225,000 books and an espresso bar. These are just two of the nation's seventeen thousand retail bookstores that account for more than $8 billion in annual sales.

While bookstores are the primary retail outlet for book sales, other outlets contribute to this market. Books are sold at college stores, department stores, grocery stores, airport terminals, chain drug stores, museums, toy and hobby shops, and at houses of worship.

How are domestic book sales handled? At a large or medium-sized publisher, its own sales staff sells the chain bookstores and the larger independent stores. Publishers also often engage jobbers, who serve as middlemen between the publisher and smaller bookstores or libraries. Sales to mass-market paperback outlets are serviced by a network of distributors and wholesalers.

When a publisher sells to a bookstore directly, the store receives a 40 to 45 percent discount from the retail price, depending upon volume, return privileges, and other factors. Until recently bookstores were able to purchase trade books from publishers on a full consignment basis, provided that they returned the books in pristine condition. Today, publishers have tightened the practice of returns.

Most publishers issue two or more catalogs a year, which are mailed directly to chains and other bookstores. The catalogs announce the current season's offerings, as well as the publisher's backlist. The purpose of these catalogs is to generate retail sales.

Some large publishers perform sales services for smaller publishers on an agreed commission basis. Simon & Schuster's catalog lists seven smaller publishers for whom it fulfills this service. In chapter 18, "Small Presses," we noted that Publishers Group West provides sales representation for a number of small presses.

International Sales

About 5 percent of U.S. trade book sales, and between 10 and 20 percent of its textbooks and professional books, are exported around the world. Although a few very large publishers maintain sales offices and warehouses abroad, most use foreign sales representative organizations to achieve these objectives. These organizations offer sales and warehousing services for many U.S. publishers in foreign countries, for which they receive an agreed commission.

Of course, as we have mentioned in chapter 11, "The Fascinating World of Subsidiary Rights," foreign publishers often purchase translation rights to U.S. and other English-language works, rather than sell the indigenous editions.

International book salespeople are often multilingual, and are thus better able to cope with the exigencies of this demanding area of publishing.

Chapter 23

◆

The Publisher's Sales Force and Sales Reps

William Morrow, a major trade book publisher headquartered in New York City, is a division of the Hearst Book Group, which in turn is a part of the giant communications organization the Hearst Corporation. Morrow and its four juvenile imprints publish about four hundred books a year. The responsibility for selling this extensive list to bookstores and other outlets rests with Morrow's trade sales department.

There are ten salespeople who work exclusively for Morrow and who cover the large book chains and independent bookstores in the major cities. To complement the efforts of its in-house sales staff, Morrow contracts with commission reps who cover the smaller territories. Reps typically handle as many as fifteen or twenty different lines of books from a number of publishers.

The Globe Pequot Press, headquartered in Connecticut, publishes about a hundred books a year, specializing in travel subjects. It has a national trade sales manager in the home office and no company-employed sales people. Instead, Globe Pequot relies on six regional reps, and one each in Canada and Europe. It also has five other reps to cover the library trade. All of its reps work on a commission basis.

Although reps often attend publishers' seasonal conferences to gain perspective on their upcoming lists of new titles, it is almost impossible for them to absorb the information from the combined output of all their publishers.

Each publisher must choose between having an exclusive sales staff, commission reps only, or a combination of the two.

CAREER TIP

Book sales, whether for a publisher directly or for a rep firm, can be a worthwhile career for the individual who enjoys selling and does not mind traveling. Salaries are similar to those in other such sales situations. Jobs are not too difficult to find. Success in this field may lead to sales manager positions at a publisher's headquarters.

What does it take to become a good book salesperson? High on the list of attributes is a love of books, but it also takes the ability to focus on a large number of new books each season. To be an effective salesperson, one must also know what kinds of books the bookseller is capable of selling, and direct his or her purchases accordingly. This function becomes increasingly significant, since booksellers don't always have the option of full return on unsold copies.

In addition to his or her sales activities, a sales rep often performs a credit and collection role. A typical conversation with a book dealer might be something like this: "I'd like to sell you our new line, but my credit department says that you paid so slowly last year, I'll have to sell you on a COD basis this year." Diplomacy and negotiation skills are the tools of a professional book salesperson.

Chapter 24

$\blacklozenge$

How Publishers Sell Books to Libraries

Today's library is an information center. At the large local public library I use, in addition to tens of thousands of books, there are a few hundred different magazines on file, and five years of *The New York Times*, the *Washington Post*, and the *Los Angeles Times* that can be accessed on microfiche.

Acquisitions are a major library function. To keep up with new releases of books, librarians read the book review sections of major newspapers, examine publishers' announcements and catalogs, and scan the industry's trade publications. In addition, they study the important review services, such as Kirkus and Booklist.

In terms of scope, there are about seventy-five thousand elementary, junior high, and high school libraries, about eighteen hundred college libraries, and almost ten thousand public libraries, with combined yearly purchases of more than $1.6 billion. The U.S. Department of Labor, Bureau of Labor Statistics, estimates that there are 150,000 people staffing these libraries.

Large universities often have a number of different libraries to facilitate their various areas of specialization.

About 70 percent of a library's purchases of books are made through library jobbers who are particularly attuned to the needs of these institutions. With access to as many as ninety thousand titles in stock, and electronic ordering capacity, a jobber is a very efficient source.

In recent years, libraries have joined in regional associations and networks in order to increase their ordering efficiency.

Chapter 25

◆

The Role of Wholesalers

A small bookstore in Seattle receives a request from a customer for a new nonfiction book, issued by a small publisher in New England, that it does not stock. If the bookstore ordered the book directly from the publisher, it might take weeks for delivery. Rather than chance losing the sale, the store places an electronic order to the Ingram Book Company, the store's principal wholesaler, and receives a same-call confirmation of the book's availability. The order is processed at Ingram's California distribution center, and the book is shipped on the same day.

How can Ingram effect such service? This wholesaler stocks two hundred thousand different titles, from sixteen hundred different publishers, including the most frequently ordered backlist items. These books are apportioned to the wholesaler's six distribution centers across the country.

Ingram maintains a computerized ordering system, as well as a telephone ordering service. Its database contains information on one million titles, the stock status of the titles in its warehouses, and the names, addresses, and phone numbers of thousands of publishers.

And, since Ingram and other wholesalers are granted a slightly higher discount from the publishers than a bookstore receives, it can still make a profit while offering books to the stores at the same price they would pay if ordered directly from the publishers.

Ingram extends its service to include inventory recommendation programs, book reference and inventory management systems, and retail promotion planning.

Baker & Taylor is another large book wholesaler with similar capabilities. In fact, its inventory is larger than Ingram's, with a stock of some ten million books. Its database includes nearly 1.2 million different titles that are updated on an average of sixty-five thousand times each month. The company also has a powerful international system, which facilitates air and ocean freight shipments to the larger export markets. Its headquarters are in North Carolina, with foreign distribution centers in Sydney, Tokyo, and London.

Libraries and schools are serviced by special jobber organizations that are attuned to the needs of these institutions. A library can reduce its paperwork substantially by ordering single copies of many different titles, and receiving one invoice from the jobber for the entire transaction.

Chapter 26

◆

The Annual Convention and Trade Exhibit of the American Booksellers Association (ABA)

At the Grand Bazaar in Istanbul, merchants in a thousand little stalls sell oriental rugs, jewelry, handicrafts, and odd-smelling confections. To the foot-weary tourist trudging down the aisles all the offerings look alike. A first-time visitor to the ABA's national convention may experience the same reaction.

The ABA convention is a four-day annual event, held at the beginning of June, and sponsored by the American Booksellers Association. It is staged each year in Chicago at the megasized McCormick Place convention center. About eighteen hundred book publisher exhibitors show their new lines of books (and some older ones as well) to a gathering of about forty-five thousand attendees, primarily booksellers, but also trade visitors and press visitors.

The booksellers attend to place orders with publishers for new books, iron out gripes they may have with publishers, meet celebrity authors, renew old acquaintances and make new ones, and, in general, be away from the store for a few days and get psyched on the book business.

Many of the booths, especially those of the larger publishers, are elaborately festooned with posters and decorations. Some of the booths have audiovisual displays. Authors abound—for signings, interviews, or just to shake hands with book buyers. At the 1995 ABA convention, about five hundred and fifty of today's leading authors signed their books. Celebrity authors present included Hillary Rodham Clinton, Gen. Colin Powell, Newt Gingrich, Hugh Downs, Larry King, Steve Allen, and Dr. Ruth peddling her new book, "Sex for Dummies."

Variety is the keynote at an ABA convention. In 1995, for example, there were more than 500 publishers of children's books, 230 publishers of reference books, 180 of religious books, 170 of gay/lesbian books, and 85 that published CD-ROM versions of books.

Highlights of any ABA convention are the conferences and events organized by the group for booksellers and publishers. In 1995, participants could attend sessions on such subjects as:

The Technical Bookstore and the Internet

Adding a Cafe to Your Bookstore?

African-American Booksellers Conference

Washington and the Bookstore

Booksellers and Publishers: Friends of Libraries

Used Books in the General Bookstore

Science Fiction & Fantasy: The Future of the Internet

Telling Lies or Telling Stories: Three Gay/Lesbian Mystery Writers Tell All

Poetry Sales & Promotions

Evenings at the ABA can be boisterous cocktail parties in hospitality suites or quiet dinners. Sales are talked about, but many are not consummated. Yet at the 1992 ABA in Anaheim, Turner Publishing came to the fair hoping to fill orders for a hundred thousand first printing of its illustrated fantasy *Dinotopia*. When the Turner people left the ABA, they had enough orders for a first printing of three hundred thousand.

Special sections at the ABA are reserved for small presses, audiovisual exhibitors, and international exhibitors. At one recent ABA convention, there were exhibits from twenty countries, including the Publishers Association of China. Large publishers are at an ABA convention as a presence; smaller ones are there for survival.

For many booksellers, the ABA is an opportunity to look at the wares of smaller publishers that do not call upon them directly and to browse at backlist titles. It's all one big literary carnival, and, for many, it's great fun.

Chapter 27

◆

The Book Retailing Revolution

In December 1994, in Encino, a posh corner of Southern California's San Fernando Valley, the superaggressive Barnes & Noble book chain opened another of its superstores, this one just a few blocks from one of its arch-competitors, the slightly smaller Super Crown. The war for dominance of the book turf continues as new stores open every week, and superstores outdo each other in service, supply, and splash.

To herald the opening of Barnes & Noble's superstore in Encino, the chain ran an expensive full-page ad in the *Los Angeles Times* boasting of the store's unique features. It would, for example, stock a hundred thousand titles as well as more than a thousand different magazines and newspapers from all over the world. A browser could curl up in an easy chair and lose him- or herself for a few minutes or a few hours with the latest gem from a favorite author, or bring the book he or she is thinking of buying to the superstore's "literary cafe" and partake of an excellent cup of Starbucks coffee while munching on a delicious pastry. The ad suggests that the cafe is an ideal setting for a "passionate literary debate."

In the store's children's section, toddlers can hang out while the bigger kids enjoy such treats as story times, puppet shows, craft exhibitions, and children's author visits.

For music lovers, this Barnes & Noble Superstore offers a selection of more than twenty-five thousand CDs, cassettes and videos, and in-store listening stations to preview selected recordings. The store also boasts a section where the computer-minded can purchase PC software, CD-ROMs, and video games.

Are Barnes & Noble and other book retail giants creating a cultural revolution? Is this the New Age of book retailing? The answer is a resounding, *yes.* Further, the effect of superstores, a phenomenon originated in 1990, may even raise the sagging national literacy levels. Says Barnes & Noble's majordomo Len Riggio, "People who are predisposed to buying books will buy more books in a greatly expanded book space . . . thus creating the idea of importance of books, of possessing books."

Let's take a closer look at the major book chains.

Barnes & Noble

Barnes & Noble was a single large bookstore on New York's lower Fifth Avenue when Len Riggio bought it in 1971. His experience until that time consisted of running contract college bookstores. In 1975, Barnes & Noble opened a forty-thousand-square-foot Sale Annex in New York and innovated such merchandising techniques as numbering best-sellers one through fifteen, and providing supermarket carts, park benches, and checkout counters.

Some years later, Barnes & Noble opened a large store on Fifth Avenue near Rockefeller Center, proceeded to gobble up Marboro Books and Bookmasters (smaller New York competitors), and acquired additional college bookstores.

Riggio, the marketing maestro who orchestrated book retailing into the twenty-first century, made his gutsiest move in 1986, when his company bought the eight-hundred-store B. Dalton Bookseller chain. Now, in addition to acquiring B. Dalton's largest bookstore on Fifth

Avenue, a few blocks from his Barnes & Noble store, he had a pocketful of debt.

At this writing, Barnes & Noble is considered the world's largest bookselling company. It owns more than thirteen hundred bookstores, including seven-hundred-odd with the B. Dalton imprimatur, almost three hundred superstores, some bearing the Bookstop and Bookstar name, 260 college stores, thirty-six Doubleday Book Shops, twelve Scribner's Bookstores, a large mail-order book business, and a specialized book publishing program. In an eight-block stretch of Fifth Avenue between 49th and 57th streets, the company owns two Doubleday stores, a thirty-three-thousand-title B. Dalton store, the venerable Scribner's, and a Barnes & Noble.

As if this rapid growth is not spectacular enough, since mid-1993 the company has been opening a new store per week. The company's annual sales volume for 1994 exceeded $1.6 billion.

Borders Group

Today, this company is the parent of Borders Book Shops, Brentano's basic bookstores, Coles bookstores, and more than eleven hundred Waldenbook stores.

The Waldenbooks story takes the "humble beginnings" prize. Larry W. Hoyt opened a small book rental library in a department store in Bridgeport, Connecticut, on March 4, 1933, the day that President Franklin D. Roosevelt was inaugurated and closed the banks. In that Depression-ridden year, the three-cents-a-day charge per book was more than many could afford, but Hoyt's modest venture prospered.

Additional rental libraries followed, primarily in department stores. By 1948, there were 250, but the "paperback explosion," with books selling for twenty-five cents each, killed the rental business. To counter this effect, Hoyt stocked both paperbacks and hardcovers on his shelves in the department stores.

In 1962, in Pittsburgh's Northway Mall, he opened his first company-owned, independent retail store. He called it The Walden Book Store (after Thoreau's "Walden Pond").

Acquired by the department store chain Carter Hawley Hale, Waldenbooks expanded rapidly and, by 1981, was the first and only bookseller to operate in all fifty states.

In 1984, Waldenbooks was bought by Kmart Corporation, the second-largest retailer in the world. The following year, the book chain opened its first Waldenbooks and More, a ten-thousand-square-foot store. The same year, it acquired the famous Globe Bookstore in Washington, D.C. In the fall of 1986, Waldenbooks opened its one thousandth bookstore.

By 1995, the chain had more than thirteen hundred stores, including eleven hundred under the Waldenbooks name. Others in the chain include Waldenbooks and More superstores, Brentano's basic bookstores, Waldenkids children's bookstores, and Borders Book Shops, a chain it acquired in 1992. In 1995, Borders was spun off from its parent, Kmart.

Crown Books

Crown Books opened for business in Rockville, Maryland, in 1977. By 1995, it had more than two hundred bookstores including Super Crown outlets in five states and Washington, D.C., with annual sales exceeding $300 million.

In part, Crown achieved this rapid growth by building large, well-stocked stores, but perhaps more likely by its aggressive policy of discounting, highlighted in its advertising with the headline, "If you paid full price, you didn't buy it at Crown Books." Crown is the first outlet I ever saw that even discounted magazines.

Crown sells the *New York Times* hardcover best-sellers at a 40 percent discount, and other hardcover books and paperbacks at 10 to 25 percent discounts. This policy could be risky, particularly on the best-sellers, since Crown only makes a few percentage points of profit on these books. But Crown's astute marketing practices have enabled it to earn respectable profits.

Crown's Super Crown stores have had rapid growth, going from six in May 1991 to seventy, four years later. These book supermarkets carry three times the number of titles of a classic Crown store. The Super Crowns feature wide aisles, roving salespeople, piped-in classical music, and Crown Kids sections with play areas for children.

A Few Words on Remainders

Recently, while browsing at my local B. Dalton store, I picked up a copy of Bob Woodward's *Veil*. The book had been published a few years ago at $21.95. I bought it for $1.49 as a remainder. A remainder is a publisher's overstock of a book that is offered to bookstores when it no longer sells at its full, or even discounted, price. B. Dalton may have bought thousands of copies of Woodward's book at fifty cents or a dollar, and is making a small profit on its sale. A good remainder section attracts buyers to a store, with the added possibility that they will also buy more expensive new titles.

The Book War for Survival: the Chains vs. the Independents

New York's Upper West Side is clearly one of the best markets for books in all of America. Independent bookstores have long established their niche in this intellectually stimulating market. One such establishment, Shakespeare & Company, is a crowded but intimate six-thousand-square-foot bookstore across the street from a block-long Barnes & Noble store that opened in spring 1983. The new Barnes & Noble threatened the existence of Shakespeare and other local stores by offering wide aisles, free gift-wrapping, substantial discounts, and, yes, the requisite espresso bar. Add to this a selection of 225,000 books and you have overwhelming competition. Commenting on the new giant bookstore phenomenon, Bill Kurland, one of the owners of Shakespeare, said that we are seeing "the Wal-Marting of America."[1]

In Denver, the respected Tattered Cover Book Store felt the pain of intrusion in 1994 when Barnes & Noble opened a thirty-five-thousand-square-foot store just a mile from its own fifty-thousand-square-foot store. At the time, Barnes & Noble already had four stores in the Denver suburbs.

There is no question that chains such as Barnes & Noble, Borders Group, Crown, and Books-A-Million (a newer chain) have proved hazardous to the health of small independent bookstores, which traditionally offer limited selections and no discounts. However, in the larger picture, the chains have promoted the sale and reading of books and have, therefore, furthered the business of book publishing.

Notes

1. Douglas Martin, "Giant Bookstore Prompts Volumes of Uneasiness," *The New York Times,* April 26, 1993, sec. B, p. 3.

◆

Chapter 28

Profile of the Tattered Cover: One of America's Largest and Best-Loved Bookstores

At the Tattered Cover in Denver, the house record for signings was set in 1992, when Persian Gulf War hero Gen. Norman Schwarzkopf signed 1,375 copies of his book *It Doesn't Take a Hero.* He did it in only three hours and three minutes. That's one every eight seconds. He even found time to pose for a photo with a toddler wearing an oversized Operation Desert Storm cap.

Readings and signings are almost daily events at this unique literary establishment. In one recent period, the Tattered Cover's book lovers could meet such a diverse group of talents as John Irving, Larry McMurtry, John Denver, baseball player Keith Hernandez, scientist Murray Gell-mann, Mikal Gilmore, Dan Quayle, and Barbara

Bush. They could also meet Gail Gilchriest, who wrote a book with the intriguing title *The Cowgirl Companion: Big Skies, Buckaroos, Honky Tonks, Lonesome Blues, and Other Glories of the True West.*

What is it about the Tattered Cover that makes it one of Denver's leading tourist attractions, even luring skiers going to and from nearby Vail and Aspen? National magazines and newspapers have written numerous articles about this book retailing phenomenon. The legendary New York book editor Jason Epstein has called the Tattered Cover, "One of the great bookstores of the Western World."[1] Let's see why it's unique.

The History

The story of the Tattered Cover is the story of its guiding spirit, Joyce Meskis. Meskis started the Tattered Cover in 1974 in a hole-in-the-wall in downtown Denver, expanded it seven times at its original site, moved it to a more spacious location across the street, and, in 1986, ultimately settled into a four-story former department store across from an upscale shopping center. Such is the loyalty of Joyce Meskis's customers that two hundred of them showed up to move books into the store's present location.

Meskis succeeded in a business that works on a minuscule profit margin (from 1 to 5 percent) by applying a management philosophy of attention to customer service and achieving the loyalty of customers and staff. Add to these factors the Tattered Cover's huge selection of books. One Boston publisher, David Godine, has said, "The Harvard Business School should have the Joyce Meskis–endowed chair of customer service and common sense."[2]

The Numbers

As of this writing, the Tattered Cover has fifty thousand square feet of retail space, stocks 220,000 different titles, and has a total of about six hundred thousand books from ninety-six hundred publishers. It employs 350 people. The store takes from 350 to 600 special orders a day, and has a switchboard with twenty-two lines, ten of them WATS lines. Although no official financial figures are issued, the Tattered Cover serves two thousand to five thousand customers a day and has an estimated annual sales volume of more than $8 million.

Almost 10 percent of the store is devoted to reduced-price books, including oversized picture books like *Day in the Life of America,* which you can buy for $19.98. There is also an extensive collection of first novels and books from small and university presses. A large area of the store is devoted to a selection of twelve hundred newspapers and magazines from the United States and abroad, including Russia, Japan, Italy, and Ireland.

The Ambiance

Lounging and comfortable browsing is encouraged at the Tattered Cover, with dozens of overstuffed chairs scattered about the store. Owner Joyce Meskis says of this policy, "It's very intentional; bookstores for many people can be intimidating places...we try to make the environment similar to their own living room, nothing too fancy, comfortable."[3]

The store's wall space is decorated with literary memorabilia and black-and-white photographs of authors. One may even run into "Charlie," a realistic full-size statue of a grandfatherly man, sitting in a chair and reading a newspaper.

Merchandising and Promotion Policies

The Tattered Cover has introduced such practices as ordering unstocked books without deposit or prepayment; an out-of-print search service, ordering books by phone, free gift wrapping, corporate and academic charge accounts, and a book registry for friends who wish to give a customer a gift.

The store has been highly innovative in its promotion. It issues a newsletter periodically highlighting new and unusual books, and also distributes *Rumpus Review,* a seasonal newsletter for children, which includes forthcoming events and book reviews written by children.

Twice-a-week children's storytimes and writing contests for young people are held.

Employee Policies

The Tattered Cover hires people from seventeen to seventy years of age. The pay scale is about the same as at other retail stores in the area—low—but employees are treated with respect, and are imbued with the store's predominant tradition of customer service. Employees undergo a two-week training program, which includes a video, "The Good, the Bad, and the OK." Some highlights: Don't correct mispronounced titles or names, don't dwell on the store being so big (people tend to root for the underdog), rise to greet a customer, and if a book isn't available, refer to another store that may have it or offer to order it. All these policies are part of Joyce Meskis's mission to make the world a better place by making readers of more people.

One industry observer commented that the Tattered Cover is a sign that an independent bookstore, when managed well, can bury the chains. The Tattered Cover and other fine independent bookstores like Portland's Powell's, Los Angeles's Book Soup, Atlanta's Oxford Book Stores, and Books and Books in Coral Gables, Florida, epitomize these formidable competitors.

Notes

1. Edwin McDowell, "Bookstore Thrives on Independence," *New York Times*, July 17, 1989, p. D2.

2. Matthew Soergel, "The Tattered Cover Novel Approach," *Rocky Mountain News*, February 4, 1990, p. 14

3. Jacqueline Johnson, "The Last Word on Bookstores," *Billings Gazette,* April 25, 1992, sec. C, p. 1.

Part V

Book Publishers' Resources

Chapter 29

---◆---

Book Publishing's Trade Publications

Publishers Weekly

*P*ublishers Weekly, or *PW* as it's known in the book trade, has been around since 1872. *PW* is the bellwether of the industry. It is read by everyone in the book publishing business and has about thirty-eight thousand paid subscribers and another sixty thousand pass-along readers. (Pass-along readers are a secondary audience composed of readers who do not actually purchase the publication.) The largest group in its subscriber mix are publishing employees, booksellers, and authors and writers.

Loyalty to a publication is largely determined by its subscription renewal rate. *PW* has a very high subscriber renewal rate, 85 percent, with an eight-year average subscription length. Few magazines, consumer or business, can match these figures.

PW's editorial package is divided into regular departments and columns, news, forecasts, and special features. One special feature, in mid-January, is "Spring Adult Announcements," which is a listing of publishers' adult trade books to be published from February to August. Another important special feature issue appears at the end of April or beginning of May, the pre-ABA and Bologna report issue. This issue typically runs about three hundred pages, and lists all the publishers participating in the forthcoming ABA Convention and their featured books. The pre-ABA issue carries advertising from 130 to 150 industry advertisers, and also serves as a convention guide.

"Positions Open" is an outstanding feature in *PW*. On the page shown opposite there are nine available jobs. Although none are entry-level positions, the others show the diversification of publishing jobs and the geographical spread of the publishers—only three are based in New York. When you are job-hunting, make sure you scan the pages of *PW.*

Daisy Maryles writes *PW*'s authoritative "Behind the Bestsellers" column, which provides coverage of this fast-paced market. She also does "My Say," and "Booksellers' Forum," readers' comments on current issues or problems facing publishing and bookselling.

Paul Nathan is a veteran *PW* columnist who writes the "rights" column. In it, Nathan reports on movie options, book club sales, and other subsidiary rights transactions.

PW is the voice of book publishing. Anyone planning to enter this field should find a library that files back issues or, better still, purchase your own subscription. At this writing, an introductory one-year subscription is $139. Call (800) 278-2991 for further information.

American Bookseller

American Bookseller is the monthly magazine of the American Booksellers Association, the sponsoring group of the annual ABA Convention. The editorial thrust of *American Bookseller* is geared to booksellers, who make up more than 70 percent of the magazine's subscribers. Each issue contains coverage of the latest trends in the industry, tips and advice on how to run bookstores, and special features on a variety of subjects, such as technical books/computer books, children's books, or business books.

WE NEED MORE SALES COVERAGE!

Woven and non-woven covering materials manufacturer needs:

Regional Sales Managers & Sales Representatives

(both experienced and trainees)
Please send your resume to:

Attn: Nancy Smith

HOLLISTON

P.O. Box 478
Kingsport, TN 37662
An Equal Opportunity Employer

ACQUISITIONS EDITOR
HBS PRESS

Reports to the Director of the Harvard Business School Press. Responsibilities for acquiring business and management titles for business executives, managers, and educators. Works with other Press editors to ensure that HBS Press manuscripts are thoughtfully analyzed and developed in relation to their appropriate markets. Assists in formulating overall marketing strategies for the list of HBS Press books with primary responsibility for his/her titles. Minimum requirements: MA or other advanced degree desirable. At least three years previous acquisitions experience in a professional or trade publishing organization. Please send resume to: Carol Franco, Harvard Business School Press, Harvard Business School Publishing, 60 Harvard Way, Boston, MA 02163. We are an Equal Opportunity Employer.

ACQUISITIONS/
DEVELOPMENTAL EDITOR

Independent press in NYC seeks editor to acquire and develop 15-20 new books in the fields of theology, religious studies and for professionals in churches, parishes and related fields. Requires degree in theology and good knowledge of parish life. Equally important is editing/publishing experience with excellent verbal and written communications skills, including the knowledge of languages. Send resume and salary history to Gwendolin Herder, Crossroad Publishing Company, 370 Lexington, Suite 2600, New York, NY 10017.

BUYER

Baker & Taylor, a leading provider of information and entertainment services worldwide, supplies books, video and audio products, software and related services to more than 100,000 bookstores, schools and public and university libraries. We're seeking an experienced Buyer to join our merchandising team. You'll be responsible for purchasing new titles placing replenishment orders, and making overstock returns for a group of publishers. As the primary liaison with the publisher, you'll also negotiate strategies to secure competitive terms, and effectively manage inventory. A Bachelor's Degree & 2-5 years book retail or wholesale buying/inventory management experience in a computerized environment required. Trade or scholarly book buying experience, and working knowledge of the E3 Trim Forecasting package a plus. We offer a competitive salary and excellent benefits package. Send resume and salary requirements to: Hope Hurley, Human Resources, Baker & Taylor, 652 East Main St, Bridgewater, NJ 08807. An Equal Opportunity/Affirmative Action Employer.

BAKER & TAYLOR

ASSOCIATE EDITOR
CORNELL UNIV. PRESS

Exceptional opportunity for individual with career commitment to scholarly publishing. Successful candidate will work closely with senior editorial staff on all aspects of manuscript acquisition, and under close supervision acquire 4-10 publishable books per year. BA required. At least two year of fulltime work experience required, preferably in book publishing. Basic computer competence essential. Please apply by letter to Roger Haydon, Acquisitions Coordinator, Cornell University Press, P.O. Box 250, Ithaca, NY 14851-0250. An AA/EOEmployer.

ASSOCIATE EDITOR

Leading theatre-cinema publisher seeks ms. editor skilled in creative line editing. Looking for expd wordsmith with passionate intelligence of subject; Goodnatured pro able to work under deadlines. Full/PT Dept. K, Applause Books, 211 W. 71st St, NYC, 10023. Fax: 212-721-2856.

COPYWRITER-SR

Simon & Schuster, the world's leading publisher serving the educational, consumer, professional, and international markets, has a challenging opportunity available in its Mass Market Division for a creative, sophisticated Copywriter. Responsibilities include writing and revising hardcover flap copy, paperback and promotion catalogue copy and coordinating administrative duties for the list. To qualify, you must have excellent communication and language skills (grammar and usage and the ability to write fluently in various mass market styles. In this quick-response department, a highly motivated efficient, flexible team player is needed who works well under deadline pressure. A liberal arts degree with 3-5 years promotional writing experience (including computer skills) in a corporate environment is preferred. To apply, please send resume with salary requirements to: J. Slaney, Simon & Schuster, 1230 Avenue of the Americas, 10th Floor, NY, NY 10020. Equal opportunity employer. m/f/d/v.

JOURNAL EDITOR

The International Reading Association seeks an editor for the Journal of Reading, a journal for adolescent and adult literacy published 8 times a year. The editor will work closely with authors, members of the editorial advisory board, and editorial, production, and marketing staff. Candidates must have a graduate degree in secondary reading, adult education, or related field, substantial editorial experience in scholarly publishing, and strong organizational, interpersonal, and communication skills. Teaching experience is a plus. Familiarity with or interest in electronic journals is desirable. The successful candidate must be willing to relocate. Send resume and salary requirements to Director of Publications, PO Box 8139, Newark, DE 19714-8139. AA/EOE.

LARGE long established East Coast based remainder co. seeking experienced sales reps. Send resume to Box PW-00223.

The biggest issues of *American Bookseller* are February and September, when the magazine covers publishers' seasonal announcements of new books, and the May pre-ABA Convention number.

American Bookseller has an important monthly feature for booksellers, "Bestsellers Around the Nation," a coast-to-coast look at the best-sellers in hardback fiction, hardback nonfiction, trade paperback, paperback fiction, and mass-market paperback.

One of my favorite *American Bookseller* features is "People in Books," which profiles an individual working in a specialized area of publishing. One recent issue had an interview with a bookseller in Prague; another, an interview with a noted literary agent.

As with *PW*, one can gain an insider's viewpoint on book publishing by reading *American Bookseller*. Most good libraries subscribe to *American Bookseller* as a guide to their book purchasing. For a subscription, write to American Bookseller, Subscription Department, 137 West 25th Street, New York, NY 10001.

Writer's Digest

Writer's Digest is the nuts-and-bolts magazine of the writing trade. It is read by freelance magazine writers, editors, authors, and would-be authors of fiction and nonfiction. Now, of course, you don't become a best-selling or even a published author by reading a monthly magazine, but in *Writer's Digest* the reader gets the practical tools that may ease the path into this demanding craft. Here are some articles from recent issues of *Writer's Digest*:

- ◆ "Avoiding the Tin Man Syndrome"—if your characters lack heart, your writing will lack readers

- ◆ "Enlighten Readers with Epiphanies"—moments of revelation can charge your fiction with energy

- ◆ "Hanging Tough with James Lee Burke"—an Edgar Award–winning mystery author tells about overcoming writer's block

- ◆ "True Crime According to the Rule"—best-selling crime author Ann Rule's tips for success

- ◆ "Creating Unreliable Narrators"—how to use narrators who are deluded, misinformed, or dishonest

- ◆ "How to Stop Cranking Out 'Puppets' and Bring Your Characters to Life"—put a fully developed character up there not one who does nothing but echo your beliefs.

Writer's Digest is a valuable guide to getting published. For information on subscriptions, write to Writer's Digest, P.O. Box 2124, Harlan, IA 51593-2313.

Book Review Sections: Must Reading for Book Professionals

If you're a librarian, bookstore buyer, book publishing professional, author, distributor, or just a book buff, book review sections and review publications are required reading.

Booksellers, particularly, devour book review sections as an advance indication of the diet of book buyers.

The New York Times Book Review

You can safely say that *The New York Times Book Review* wins the award for circulation and clout. As a supplement to the *Sunday Times*, it reviews about fifty books a week, of which about thirty receive significant attention. A favorable review on page one can send a book's sales spiraling.

Although there are, perhaps, as many unfavorable reviews as there are raves, the editors are nonetheless selective in the kind of books they review. Original paperbacks, for example, receive second-hand treatment, as does good-read popular fiction.

With a Sunday readership of about two million, you can easily realize the impact of *The New York Times Book Review.* Become familiar with the publication even while you're still in college. Most good libraries file it, and you can receive it by subscription for $52 a year. Call (800) 631-2580 for information.

Other Review Sections and Publications

There are, of course, other important Sunday newspaper review sections. The *Los Angeles Times*, the *Washington Post*, and the *Chicago Tribune* publish fine Sunday book review supplements.

The American Library Association publishes the highly regarded *Booklist*, primarily as an authoritative review service for libraries and bookstores.

Library Journal, a bimonthly for librarians, reviews more than two hundred books per issue. Reviews are done by libraries across the country. Each issue also carries a CD-ROM review, video reviews, and audio reviews.

Publishers Weekly carries abbreviated but well-grounded reviews in each of its weekly issues. The *Kirkus Review* is a long-respected source of reviews for libraries and bookstores.

The *New York Review of Books*, as its title indicates, is a review publication sold by subscription to an audience of enlightened readers. In addition to reviews, the *Review* contains articles, often controversial, about authors and issues.

Many magazines carry book reviews, particularly the so-called class publications: *Harper's Magazine*, the *New Republic*, the *New Yorker*, the *Atlantic*, and the *Nation*.

In addition to the eager readers of reviews among the public, the publishing industry constantly monitors reviews in publications as a guide to what it is going to publish in the future. When a publisher receives a good review for one of its own books, that book is promoted and publicized to bookstores and the public to gain maximum exposure.

Movie producers are eager readers of reviews, especially of fiction works, with the idea of turning them into films. Of course, when a publisher owns a manuscript that he or she thinks will make a good movie, it is shown to producers months before it is published and reviewed.

Chapter 30

♦

Book Publishing's Largest Information and Reference Company

R R. Bowker, a division of Reed Reference Publishing, which in turn is a division of Reed International, one of the world's leading publishing and information companies, publishes *Books in Print* and *Literary Market Place*. Reed International also owns the Cahners Group, which publishes seventy magazines, including *Publishers Weekly, Library Journal, Variety*, and *Interior Design*.

If you're in publishing, bookselling, or library work, Bowker's reference works are of inestimable value. Let's look at a few of these sources.

Books in Print

Did you ever wonder where to find information on some obscure book that you're not sure is still in print? The ten-volume set *Books in Print* solves that problem by providing the current price, edition, publisher, binding, and author information on more than one million books. Tens of thousands of new titles are added each year. Publishers make constant reference to *Books in Print*, often just to check the competition's output. Large bookstores may have a set of *Books in Print* for reference purposes.

Books in Print Online provides an on-line service for libraries and bookstores enabling them to access information in *Books in Print* with microcomputer speed and convenience. This information is also available in CD-ROM, microfiche, and tape.

Books in Print Plus contains more than 230,000 current full-text book reviews from *Library Journal*, *Publishers Weekly*, *Booklist*, *Kirkus*, and other leading review sources, all on the same CD-ROM.

Subject Guide to Books in Print indexes more than 875,000 nonfiction titles from *Books in Print* under more than seventy-seven thousand Library of Congress subject headings.

Literary Market Place

In Bowker's annual directory *Literary Market Place (LMP)* you can find listings and profiles of all major book publishers, book clubs, associations, suppliers to the book business, and more. A key feature is *LMP*'s "Names and Numbers" section, which has current contact information of twenty thousand key people in the industry. *LMP*'s latest edition has two thousand pages. With *LMP*, you can reach the people who publish, package, review, represent, edit, translate, typeset, illustrate, design, print, bind, promote, publicize, ship, and distribute books. For those dealing with the foreign market, Bowker also publishes *International Literary Market Place (ILMP)*.

If you are entering the publishing profession, become familiar with its reference tools. Most libraries have *Books in Print* and *LMP*. These sources of information can be extremely helpful in research and writing projects, and even prove beneficial in preparing you for a job interview or identifying contacts.

For information about R. R. Bowker or any of its publications write to: R. R. Bowker, 245 West 17th Street, New York, NY 10011.

Part VI

The Publishing Job Scene

Chapter 31

$\blacklozenge$

Where to Go to Study Publishing

I f you polled all the employees at Farrar, Straus & Giroux or Random House, it's doubtful that more than 10 percent pursued college programs in publishing or majored in English. Industry leader Samuel S. Vaughan, former president of Doubleday, refutes the common conviction that publishing is the place for people who like books.

> *There is nothing wrong with having an English major or with liking books, except that neither is a sufficient qualification for entering the publishing field. Better prerequisites are to be passionately persuaded about print, committed to the power of the word, in love with both the idea of books and the ideas in books, in love with language, capable of enduring frustration, and possessing a taste for long odds.[1]*

Vaughan counsels beginners with the advice that editorial work is just one of many immensely interesting jobs in publishing, and general trade books only a slice of the industry. To succeed in these jobs, it isn't necessary to major in publishing in college. However, in today's competitive marketplace specialized training may help get that first job or speed the advancement process once you're employed.

From an educational standpoint, there are three sources for this preparation: undergraduate publishing or related majors, summer book publishing programs, and college extension courses. We'll look at each.

Graduate and Undergraduate Programs in Publishing

The following is a list of colleges and universities with majors and/or courses in publishing and its allied fields:

Arkansas State University
City University of New York
Columbia University
Florida State University
George Washington University
Hofstra University
Kent State University
New York City Community College
New York University
Northeastern University
Oregon State University
Rice University
Rochester Institute of Technology
Sarah Lawrence College
School of Visual Arts (New York)
Simmons College
Southern Illinois University
State University of New York (Albany, Geneseo, and Old Westbury)

Syracuse University
University of Alabama
University of California (Berkeley)
University of Chicago
University of Connecticut
University of Denver
University of Illinois
University of Iowa
University of Kansas
University of Kentucky
University of New Mexico
University of Southern California
University of Tennessee
West Virginia University

Summer Publishing Programs

A number of colleges conduct comprehensive summer publishing programs. New York University, Radcliffe, and Stanford combine magazine and book publishing, while the University of Denver only has a book publishing program. All are expensive and require a commitment of four to six weeks. However, these programs can be extremely productive in helping to build a career in these professions. Admission to any of the four programs is highly selective and competitive. We suggest early application.

Summer Publishing Institute, New York University

Having written the magazine portion for the first joint magazine and book program in 1980, I am obviously partial to New York University's Summer Publishing Institute. The institute runs for seven intensive weeks each summer in New York City, the publishing capital of the world, and combines both magazine and book publishing. All students are required to take both programs. Each segment—book and magazine—consists of morning, afternoon, and optional evening and Saturday sessions, field trips, and panel discussions. Students learn the fundamentals of publishing through lectures. In a typical program, about forty book industry leaders participate, along with forty from the magazine field.

Highlighting the program are the skill development workshops, where students tackle the nuts-and-bolts aspects of publishing. Assignments are critiqued and graded. In simulations, students are organized into teams and engage in such sophisticated practices as evaluating manuscripts, bidding for the rights to projects they wish to publish, developing marketing plans, and, finally, presenting their proposed list of books at a sales conference.

The Summer Publishing Institute helps students in the job hunt, including participation in a job fair, which gives students an opportunity to meet and interview with major book and magazine firms. Field trips to publishers and their resources are arranged. Summer Publishing Institute certificates are awarded to students who complete the seven-week program.

As two recent graduates put it, "The Institute actually helped me find a job as soon as the program ended," and, "The Institute really is where publishers go to look for new talent in the business."

The program at New York University's Summer Publishing Institute runs for seven weeks. Dormitory housing at the university is available at moderate rates. It's a worthwhile investment. For information on New York University's Summer Publishing Institute, call (212) 988-7219.

Radcliffe Publishing Course

The Radcliffe Publishing Course is the granddaddy of all summer publishing programs, having originated in 1948. It has been referred to by students and lecturers as "the shortest graduate school in the world." The course runs for six weeks each summer and combines a book and magazine program.

Students at the course learn the publishing craft from a faculty of ninety or more professionals who describe the nature of their work, conduct workshops, and answer questions in classroom discussions and informal sessions.

Students form magazine workshop groups for two weeks. The objective here is to develop an original concept for a new magazine. At the conclusion of the workshop, students present their magazine prospectuses and business plans to industry professionals for evaluation.

In small workshops held throughout the course, students learn the fundamentals of copyediting, manuscript evaluation, and magazine editing.

In a week-long book workshop, students from publishing "companies" develop lists for publication. Editing, evaluation, design, promotion, subsidiary rights, and marketing come into play in this process.

Students at the course are required to live on campus, which enables them to meet with speakers informally at dinner, and work on assignments after class hours. A week after the course ends, two career fairs are held, one in Boston and one in New York. The course is expensive and limited to college graduates. For information, write to Radcliffe Publishing Course, 77 Brattle Street, Cambridge, MA 02138, (617) 495-8678.

Stanford Professional Publishing Course

The Stanford Professional Publishing Course is limited to 165 publishing professionals, with a minimum of three years' experience. Those fortunate to qualify are rewarded with an exceptional program. It runs for thirteen days each July and covers both book and magazine publishing.

Course participants indicate their interest in either discipline—book or magazine—and attend workshops in general sessions, as well as the track they have preselected. About sixty publishing professionals, including many heads of companies, make up the faculty for the course. Outstanding faculty members from Stanford's graduate schools appear as guest lecturers.

An integral part of the course is a case project developed by the students and presented to the faculty on the final day.

Many companies from both the United States and abroad have sponsored employees to attend the course. Low-cost, on-campus accommodations are available. For information, write to Stanford Professional Publishing Course, Bowman Alumni House, Stanford, CA 94305, (415) 723-0544

University of Denver Publishing Institute

Publishing veteran Esther Margolis says of the Denver Institute, "Four weeks at Denver equals a half a year entry level at a publishing house."[2]

The University of Denver Publishing Institute is a concentrated four-week, full-time course devoted exclusively to book publishing. Elizabeth Geiser, co-director of Denver's Publishing Institute since it began in 1976, comments on her program.

Interview

What do students want?

To bring great literature to the masses...fine, but you've got to run a profitable business.

What do you want?

To be sure the three major functions of publishing are represented: editing, marketing, and production. I also want to be sure that all phases of publishing (such as) scholarly, textbook, trade, paperback, and children's are represented.

What do you try to teach?

A balance between self-confidence and an openness to learn. I tell them the most important factor in a first job is not (the size of) the company, but the person you work for. Look for a mentor.

For information on the University of Denver Publishing Institute, call (303) 871-2570 or write to Publishing Institute, 2075 S. University Boulevard, #D-114, Denver, Colorado, 80210.

College Book Publishing Programs

Many colleges offer book publishing seminars, workshops, and programs. Most are listed in *Peterson's Guide to Book Publishing Courses*. Here are a few well-known programs and some typical courses.

The University of Chicago Publishing Program

The University of Chicago Press is one of the largest academic presses in the nation, with an output of about 250 books a year and a backlist of almost four thousand books. The University of Chicago also conducts an outstanding academic publishing program for professionals and recent graduates. The program's courses are largely taught by the staff of the University of Chicago Press.

The program offers quarter-long courses, short seminars, and one-day workshops for working professionals from the field of publishing. It also offers a year-long introduction to publishing, consisting of three quarter-long courses: basic manuscript editing, introduction to book or magazine design, and introduction to book or magazine production.

After the first year, the program offers a second year specialization in writing, editing, and production.

A typical course in the program's curriculum is "Freelancing in Publishing: The Career Potential." This course is taught by three editors who have made freelancing their careers, and explores the many issues involved with self-employment, as well as the specific opportunities in this increasingly popular area.

The University of Chicago's year-long sequences are geared to recent college graduates planning to enter publishing, as well as those working in other fields eager to make a change.

For information on this outstanding program, write to Stephanie Meedlock, Director, Publishing Program, 5835 Kimbark Avenue, Chicago, IL 60637-1608, (312) 702-1682.

City University of New York Publishing Program

Courses in this program include "The Profession of Literary Agent: A Workshop," "Selling Subsidiary Rights," "Marketing and Sales for the Non-Specialist," and "Copyediting and Proofreading Workshop." For information, write to Education in Publishing Program, City University Graduate Center, 33 West 42nd Street, New York, NY 10036.

New York University Book Publishing Certificate Program

New York University conducts a diploma program in book publishing. Courses include "Editorial Processes and Procedures," "Elements of Production," and "Organization and Management in Publishing." Completing six courses is required for achieving the certificate. Write to Diploma Program in Book Publishing, New York University, Two University Place, New York, NY 10003.

Writers Conferences and Workshops

One cannot expect to attend a four-week writing workshop and emerge as a skilled writer. Becoming a writer is a long process involving infinite hours of reading, as well as studying and analyzing the techniques of professionals. Along with creative writing courses at the college level, such workshops will, however, nurture one's talent. Then it's a case of writing, writing, and more writing.

Most colleges offer excellent writing programs. However, attendance at a good writer's conference or workshop is additionally helpful because of the opportunity to meet successful authors. At times, a mentor relationship may be established. Just being immersed in this environment may spark creativity.

Literary Market Place (LMP) lists about 170 writers' conferences and workshops, many conducted during the summer. We list just a few of them and suggest that the reader consults *LMP* for names, addresses, and schedules.

Annual Black Writers'
Conference
Black Writers Workshop
Committee
5312 Mormandie
Oakland, CA 94619
(415) 532-6719

Aspen Writers' Conference
Box 7726
Aspen, CO 81612
(303) 925-3122

Bennington Writing Workshops
Bennington College
Bennington, VT 05201
(802) 442-5401

Bread Loaf Writers' Conference
Middlebury College
Middlebury, VT 05753
(802) 388-3711, ext. 5286

Chautauqua Writers' Workshop
Chautauqua Summer School
Box 1098
Chautauqua, NY 14722
(716) 357-6232

Children's Book Writing and
Illustration Workshops
Robert Quackenbush Studios
460 East 79th Street
New York, NY 10021
(212) 744-3822

Clarion Workshop in Science
Fiction and Fantasy Writing
Michigan State University,
Lyman Briggs School
E-28 Holmes Hall
East Lansing, MI 48825-1107
(517) 353-6486

Duke University Writers'
Conference
Duke University, The Bishop's
House
Durham, NC 27708
(919) 684-6259

Harvard Summer Writing
Program
Harvard University Div. of
Continuing Education
Dept. One, 20 Garden Street
Cambridge, MA 02138
(617) 495-2921

Hofstra University Summer
Writers' Conference
Continuing Ed. Department
Memorial Hall, Room 232
Hempstead, NY 11550
(516) 560-5016

Romance Writers of America
National Conference
Romance Writers of America
13700 Veterans Memorial Drive,
Suite 315
Houston, TX 77014
(713) 440-6885

Barnaby Conrad
Santa Barbara Writers
Conference
Box 304
Carpinteria, CA 93014
(805) 684-2250

Wesleyan Writers Conference
Wesleyan University
Middletown, CT 06457
(203) 347-9411

Attending a summer publishing or extension program, or writers' conference, involves time and money. However, I do believe the rewards in terms of preparation for a career in book publishing or in training to become a writer make the commitment worthwhile.

Notes

1. Samuel S. Vaughan, *Guide to Book Publishing Courses* (New York: Peterson's Guides, 1979).

2. John Allison, "Publishing's Ms. Chips," *American Bookseller* (April 1989): 64.

Chapter 32

───────── ◆ ─────────

Tips on Breaking into Book Publishing

A recent study by the U.S. Bureau of Labor Statistics offers a bleak outlook for all college graduates hitting the job market. Their findings include these hard facts:

◆ The average weekly wage for all twenty- to twenty-four-year-olds regardless of educational level dropped 7.4 percent during the past ten years when adjusted for inflation.

◆ Of college graduates below the age of twenty-four, 91.3 percent were employed. However, one-fifth were employed in jobs beneath their educational level.

If there is difficulty finding any job after graduation, the competition is even fiercer for getting a job in book publishing. The candidate for a first job needs to employ all the skills and tricks he or she can muster and, because publishing is a high-profile field, the job approach must be more strategic than in other industries.

At an annual meeting of the book industry's Association of American Publishers, people at different levels in book publishing were asked how they got their first jobs in this field. Here are some of the responses:

- ◆ I volunteered.
- ◆ Help wanted ad.
- ◆ By knocking on lots of doors.
- ◆ By accident.
- ◆ I'm a member of the family.
- ◆ Through and as a student at NYU.
- ◆ Eleven rejections and an acceptance.
- ◆ Through my college placement service.
- ◆ I was asked.
- ◆ Off the street.
- ◆ Through an endless chain of tenuous connections.
- ◆ I bought the company.

Twenty Tips on How to Break Into Publishing

1. *Educate yourself about the business.* Read everything you can find about book publishing. Read the important trade publications in this field (see chapter 29). A year's back issues of *Publishers Weekly* contain a plethora of information about every phase of publishing.

2. *Attend a summer publishing program.* In chapter 31 we discussed a number of these programs. Some combine book and magazine publishing. These programs are expensive, but may prove to be worthy investments.

3. *Target your prospects.* Decide for yourself whom you want to work for and in what publishing specialization. Examine the latest *Literary Market Place (LMP)* in your library for names and addresses of the target companies.

4. *Prepare for your interview.* If you are in a school that has a good placement department, find out if they can set up some role-playing situations with specific advice on handling an interview. Just getting an interview is a foot in the door. Once you've secured an interview, prepare for it carefully. Organize your thinking and review the information you have on the company. Be articulate, self-confident, and enthusiastic. Talk about yourself—what you've learned, what you offer, and what you can do for Publisher X. Don't try to recite everything you know. Selectivity shows you are thinking. Come to the interview with some knowledge about the publisher's business.

5. *Meet with recruiters when they visit your campus.* Ask questions and try to learn their hiring practices, standards, and so forth. Attend job fairs.

6. *Take any entry-level job you can get.* Even if you are determined to become an editor, start in a noneditorial job if it's available. You may be able to switch later or apply for an editorial job with another publisher.

7. *Ask about a company's training program.* Many publishers don't have this important feature. It's clearly a bonus if they do have a program.

8. *Use personal contacts.* They are your best sources for job leads. Personal referrals are most advantageous. Contact your college's alumni association, which may enable you to track people from your school who have gone to work at a company that interests you.

9. *Don't fret about rejection.* It is no cause to suppose that you will not qualify elsewhere. Consider your job hunt as a learning experience. Perseverance will win you the opportunity to begin your publishing career.

10. *Internships give you a step ahead.* A large percentage of interns are hired for full-time jobs. Many large companies are identifying potential interns as early as their college freshman year, so apply early. If possible, choose an internship at a company that has an intern supervision program. If you do

the internship between your junior and senior years, you can keep in touch with your mentor all through your senior year.

11. *Read any current books you can find about the publishing business.* They may contain information about getting started.

12. *Attend job fairs.* If publishers participate, ask specific questions about hiring procedures and company policies.

13. *Take extension courses.* Even if you are working at a publishing or other job in New York, take one of the fine extension courses at New York University or the School of Visual Arts.

14. *Learn the techniques of cold-calling.* You'll probably get your first job by cold-calling, letter writing, or networking. Make sure you are adept at each.

15. *Focus on the large publishers discussed in chapter 35.* These companies often have training programs and provide educational benefits.

16. *Get a graduate degree in business.* It's important if you wish to reach for the gold, but it may be a good idea to work in the field for a couple of years and then, with your company's permission, take a leave of absence. Many companies encourage this practice.

17. *Go the recruiter route.* Few professional recruiters specialize in publishing. Here is a list of some that do:

Helen Akullian Agency
280 Madison Avenue
New York, NY 10016
(212) 532-3210

Lynne Palmer
14 East 60th Street
New York, NY 10022
(212) 759-2942

Winston Personnel
535 Fifth Avenue
New York, NY 10017
(212) 557-5000

Gardner Personnel, Inc.
300 Madison Avenue
New York, NY 10017
(212) 687-6615

Bert Davis Associates
425 Madison Avenue
New York, NY 10017
(212) 838-4000

✓ Roth Young of Chicago
3330 West Dundee, Unit C8
Northbrook, IL 60062
(708) 509-8801

18. *Read the industry's trade publications. Publishers Weekly is a* must read (see chapter 29 for other publications). Most good libraries have them on file.

19. *Create a good résumé.* A good résumé should sell you. It should exude a sense of energy. Highlight your relevant skills. Reflect your talents, interests, and the benefits you will bring to your prospective employer. Keep it neat, clear, and precise. Tailor your résumé to each position you apply for. Don't waste space on clubs you belonged to in high school. Since it's a book publishing job you're applying for, your punctuation, spelling, and production of the résumé must be perfect. If you have won any awards for educational excellence or leadership, detail them. Also, list your computer skills, even though most graduates know how to use a personal computer. Dozens of books have been written about how to write a résumé. Many will serve you well in crafting an effective résumé. My own favorite is Arco's *Résumés That Get Jobs*, the all-time best-selling résumé book. See the following example of an entry-level résumé.

20. *Take pains with each cover letter.* Don't blow the impact of a good résumé with a bad cover letter. Together they create a first impression of you. Stay clear of the form letter. Let them know why you're interested and why you think you're right for them. Pay special attention to spelling, typos, and grammar. Cover letters should be short. Say just what you want: an interview.

How to Handle Interviews

◆ Dress appropriately and conservatively. Don't be afraid to smile. Show a genuine interest in the employer's operations, and ask questions about the company.

◆ If you are applying for a specific job, be prepared to ask hard questions about the job and all its duties.

◆ Expect your interviewer to ask questions about your education, background, and previous jobs.

213

Sample Cover Letter

Ellen C. Wagner
330 Main Street
Anytown, NY 00000
(516) 555-1234

September 25, 1995

Ms. Iris Forbes
Vice President, Human Resources
Giles Publishing Company
905 Third Avenue
New York, NY 10023

Dear Ms. Forbes:

As my enclosed résumé shows, I am a recent graduate of Hofstra University with a major in English. My experience includes an internship with a large publishing company and word processing a novel for a major author.

I would like to meet with you to discuss an entry-level editorial job with your company, and I will call on Monday, October 3rd, to arrange an interview.

I look forward to meeting you.

Sincerely,

Ellen C. Wagner

Enclosure

Sample Résumé

Ellen C. Wagner
330 Main Street
Anytown, NY 00000
(714) 555-1234

OBJECTIVE: To obtain employment in book publishing that allows me to use my language and writing skills.

EDUCATION: B.A. English, summa cum laude, Hofstra University, Hempstead, NY, May 1995.

Concentration in book publishing. Courses included theory and practice of publishing, book editing, book design and production, the economics of publishing. Summer workshop in book publishing (intensive four-week program) School of Continuing Education, New York University, New York, NY, July 1995.

EXPERIENCE: Served as editor of *Hofstra Literary Magazine*; awarded second place in the national competition of Association of American Publishers. Phoenix Press: New York, NY. Paid internship, May through August 1994. Participated in rotating internship program. Helped prepare final edited copy for electronic typesetting. Assisted publicity director in planning and organizing authors' tours. Aided the production manager in installing a desktop production system.

Word-processed manuscript for author Janice Brandon, Southampton, NY. Paid assignment, July through August 1993.

Professional references available.

- ◆ Ask about perks, benefits, and tuition reimbursement—but don't ask about the retirement plan.

- ◆ Within twenty-four hours after an interview, send your interviewer a follow-up letter. This is an excellent chance to reiterate your interest in the position and express your appreciation for his or her time. Good luck.

- ◆ Sell yourself in the interview. Once you get your foot in the door, it's up to you.

- ◆ Create a feeling of self-confidence the moment you enter the interviewer's office. A well-known employment specialist states that the first five minutes of the interview usually determine whether you are hired.

- ◆ Know what you've got to sell and be able to convince the interviewer that you've got the necessary assets and abilities for the job.

- ◆ Be prepared for any questions the interviewer might ask you about his or her company.

What Impresses an Interviewer Most

In my book *Making It in Public Relations*, I reported the comments of a group of seasoned professionals on what they valued in people seeking to break into the field. Their answers offer insight into the experience and characteristics needed to get started in any creative pursuit:

- ◆ Self-confidence, knowledge of the humanities, interest in business.

- ◆ Sincerity—the candidate's desire to learn from the bottom up.

- ◆ Ability to manage time.

- ◆ Brainpower and intellect.

- ◆ Candor.

- ⧫ Crystal-clear and orderly speech, suggesting an orderly mind.

- ⧫ Ability to listen, as well as converse.

- ⧫ Demeanor and dress.

- ⧫ The gray matter he/she has, an eagerness to learn.

- ⧫ The questions he/she asks.

- ⧫ Evidence of intelligence and motivation.

- ⧫ The preparation the candidates have made for the interviews.

The media specialist Roger Bumstead contributes these additional thoughts on what turns him off in an interview:

> *Candidates without a career focus; candidates who want me to do the talking; candidates who "laze" in the chair across from me; candidates who are either boring or arrogant; candidates who don't dress properly because they think it doesn't matter when they're seeing a recruiter. Wow, are they wrong!* [1]

Wise Words from Industry Leader Richard Curtis

Richard Curtis has been in book publishing for more than twenty-five years, joining the noted Scott Meredith Literary Agency right after graduation, where he was foreign rights manager for seven years. He launched a freelance writing career in 1967 and has had some fifty of his books published by many major houses. Today, Richard Curtis represents close to two hundred authors in all fields and reports more than $6 million in annual sales for his authors.

He is a member of many industry groups and is the agent for the Science Fiction Writers of America and a member of the National Writers Union. Here are some of Curtis's random thoughts on book publishing today:

The traditional book industry and its publishers are losing ground to television, movies, and computerized entertainment such as video games. Interestingly enough, it is also to those fields that publishers are looking for their salvation.

Because the surviving publishers are all vying for a small number of potentially best-selling books and star authors, the number of trade books (general interest fiction and nonfiction) published annually is definitely shrinking.

There are still good entry-level jobs in publishing, and enough fluidity so that a young editor can advance to a senior position relatively quickly. If you're willing to think beyond the limitations of the conventional publishing and bookselling fields, you may be able to help the industry expand again in some very exciting ways.

The most interesting book-related activity is now in the field of electronic media. Books that can be delivered to readers or "viewers" on disk or over phone or cable lines will, I confidently predict, become the principal way that future generations will access information and "edutainment."

Traditional publishers realize this and have begun to develop multimedia capability or join forces with companies that produce it.

Therefore, young people must steep themselves in computer technology and electronic media. They can get jobs in those media. But if they are keen to be in publishing, they will be armed with skills that are useful and desirable to an industry that must go electronic if it is to survive.

In other words, an editor with a grammar book, dictionary, and blue pencil will be at a distinct disadvantage against one who knows how to operate a computer or CD-ROM and communicate over an on-line network.

Cogent thoughts indeed from an industry leader.

Note

1. Leonard Mogel, *Making It in Advertising* (New York: Collier Books, 1993).

Chapter 33

◆

The Increasingly Dominant Role of Women in Book Publishing

The evidence is clear. In most areas of book publishing, except at the very top level, women are still making less money than men for doing the same jobs. But this situation is changing. Each year we see women's compensation coming closer to parity with men. And perhaps of more importance, women are being given the opportunity to hold leadership positions.

On the editorial side of publishing, women now have an equal share of the top jobs, and at the business and corporate level, women are closing the gap.

It is always embarrassing to make up a list of women or minorities who have succeeded in a particular profession. It smacks of

221

tokenism. Yet it does serve a purpose, offering encouragement to those coming into the field, and a realization that just below these leaders are dozens of middle-management publishing professionals poised for that rapid move to the corner office.

The former publisher of Random House, Joni Evans, has said: "The great thing about publishing is that it's entrepreneurial...if you signed up a best-seller, or edited it, or sold the subsidiary rights, you would get a report card quickly."[1]

Here is a partial list of those who have made it to top managerial positions at this writing:

> Carole Baron—President and Publisher, Dell Publishing
>
> Maureen Egan—Publisher, Warner Paperback Books
>
> Phyllis Grann—President and CEO, the Putnam Berkley Group
>
> Linda Grey—President, Ballantine Publishing Group
>
> Barbara Grossman—Publisher, Viking Penguin
>
> Alice Mayhew—Vice President and Editorial Director, Simon & Schuster Trade Division
>
> Susan Petersen—Publisher, Riverhead Books (Putnam)
>
> Michelle Sidrane—Executive Vice President and Publisher, Crown (Random House)
>
> Nan Talese—Senior Vice President, Doubleday
>
> Susan Weinberg—Vice President and Managing Director, Quality Paperback Book Club
>
> Ellen Crowley—Vice President and Publisher, Gale Research

The Women's National Book Association

The Women's National Book Association (WNBA) was established in 1917 in New York City by a group of fifteen women who were refused admission to the annual booksellers' convention. Their purpose was to organize women who worked in all branches of the book industry, and to support the role of women in the profession.

Since that time the group has grown to an organization of almost a thousand members, with active chapters in New York, Boston, Nashville, Binghamton, Detroit, San Francisco, Los Angeles, Atlanta, Dallas, and Washington, D.C.

What is unique about the WNBA is the diversity of its membership, which includes publishers, booksellers, writers, editors, agents, designers, illustrators, and book and magazine producers.

The WNBA defines its role as follows:

◆ Serves as a network for professionals in the field.

◆ Provides a forum for exchange of ideas and information.

◆ Generates contacts and connections at all career levels.

◆ Promotes recognition of women's achievements in the book world.

For further information about this important organization, write or call WNBA, 160 Fifth Avenue, New York, NY 10010, (212) 675-7805.

Notes

1. Edwin McDowell, "Women Move to the Top in Publishing," *The New York Times,* October 25, 1987, sec D, p 24.

Chapter 34

---◆---

Job Opportunities in Book Publishing Outside New York

The "People" page of *Publishers Weekly* lists promotions within one publisher's organization, as well as job shifts from one company to another. Job shifting in book publishing is as customary as it is in the fields of magazine publishing, advertising, and broadcasting. People move in order to achieve greater responsibility, the opportunity for promotion, and to earn more money.

Making It in Book Publishing Outside New York

New York City has Bloomingdale's, Soho, Tribeca, Columbus Avenue, and free concerts in Central Park. New York is also the headquarters of many of the largest book publishers, but it is a very expensive place to live, particularly on beginners' publishing salaries.

Are there enough publishers in other parts of the country so that you can establish a career outside of Gotham? Yes. Here are some large publishing houses and their locations:

♦ Addison-Wesley Publishing Co., Reading, Massachusetts

♦ Andrews and McMeel, Kansas City, Missouri

♦ Augsburg Fortress, Publishers, Minneapolis, Minnesota

♦ Brassey's, McLean, Virginia

♦ Cliffs Notes, Lincoln, Nebraska

♦ Wm. B. Eerdmans Publishing Co., Grand Rapids, Michigan

♦ Encyclopaedia Britannica, Chicago, Illinois

♦ Harper San Francisco, San Francisco, California

♦ Houghton Mifflin, Boston, Massachusetts

♦ Macmillan Publishing USA, Indianapolis, Indiana

♦ Meredith Books, Des Moines, Iowa

♦ C. V. Mosby, St. Louis, Missouri

♦ Microsoft Press, Redmond, Washington

♦ National Textbook Co., Lincolnwood, Illinois

♦ Thomas Nelson Publishers, Nashville, Tennessee

♦ Sunset Books, Menlo Park, California

♦ Western Publishing, Racine, Wisconsin

♦ Word, Dallas, Texas

In addition to this list, there are many smaller publishing services and university presses across the nation. Consult *Literary Market Place* for a complete list of American publishers, their specialties, and addresses.

Chapter 35

———— ◆ ————

The Twenty Largest Publishers

S imon & Schuster is the world's largest publishing organization, with about ten thousand employees and yearly revenues of $2 billion. Its various divisions publish trade, educational, business, and technical books. When looking for a job in book publishing, it is helpful to know who are the largest publishers. Here is a list of the twenty largest publishing groups, listed according to the parent company's name and relative ranking in terms of revenues:

1. Simon & Schuster

2. Time Publishing Group

3. Harcourt Brace Jovanovich (Harcourt General)

4. Random House

5. Reader's Digest

6. McGraw-Hill

7. Encyclopaedia Britannica

8. Bantam Doubleday Dell (Bertelsmann)

9. The Thomson Group

10. Times Mirror

11. HarperCollins

12. Grolier

13. Macmillan Publishing USA

14. Houghton Mifflin

15. Western Publishing

16. World Book Encyclopedia

17. John Wiley

18. Penguin USA

19. Putnam Group

20. St. Martin's

Consult *Literary Market Place* for addresses of these companies and the names of their key personnel.

The Case for Large versus Small Publishers

A large publishing house is likely to have in-house training programs, educational benefits, and the opportunity to learn from the industry's brightest talents and to witness high-profile publishing develop. The downside: As a result of bigness, you may end up feeling pigeon-holed, stymied, or unrecognized.

At a small house, salaries across the board are lower than they are with the big guys. Also, a small publisher has fewer personnel and calls on its people to go beyond their job descriptions. The learning process may be accelerated, but the disciplines that should accompany the learning are lacking.

Ultimately, when you are job-hunting, the choice is governed by the opportunities in the marketplace and, in the final analysis, it comes down to ability and personality. If you're resourceful and smart, you'll make it at a large or small publisher.

When we're dealing with *trade* publishers only, the list of the ten largest is as follows:

1. Random House
2. Bantam Doubleday Dell
3. Simon & Schuster
4. HarperCollins
5. Penguin USA
6. Time Warner Trade
7. Putnam Berkley
8. Hearst Trade Group
9. St. Martin's
10. Houghton Mifflin

Random House, at the top of the list, has yearly sales of about $1.2 billion, while Houghton Mifflin, at the bottom, has sales of about $100 million.

Chapter 36

◆

Internships and Training Programs: Hiring Hints from Human Resources Chiefs

C ompany policies regarding internships and training programs vary a great deal. The nation's largest publisher, Simon & Schuster, does not have an organized internship program. Farrar, Straus & Giroux has unpaid internships year-round on a flexible schedule. If an opportunity exists for an internship at a publisher such as Farrar, Straus, by all means take it, especially while you're still in college and preferably between your sophomore and junior year. In numerous situations, unpaid interns have been hired by publishers for paid jobs.

Find out if the company you are applying to has an on-site internship supervisor. It is an important asset to a company's program.

You must send a résumé and cover letter to apply for an internship. Follow the same procedure as if you were applying for a regular job. Often an interview is required for internships. Consider the interview as a major opportunity. Ask questions. Discuss your duties. Follow up the interview with a thank-you letter.

Although it is difficult to get *any* job at a book publisher, find out if the publisher you are applying to has a training program. It is worth the extra effort to get a job at a publisher that has a tradition of training. Publishers use these programs as a way of discovering and nurturing bright young stars.

Hiring Policies of Major Publishing Companies

Farrar, Straus & Giroux
19 Union Square West
New York, NY 10003
(212) 741-6900
Contact: Peggy Miller

Internships: The company offers an unpaid internship program of varying duration. The closing date for applications for the summer program is mid-April. Phone for an appointment.

Employment: Send résumé when applying for a full-time job. A personal interview is required.

Houghton Mifflin Company
222 Berkeley Street
Boston, MA 02116
(617) 351-5000

Internships: The company has an extremely limited number of summer internships available, predominantly for high school seniors or college freshmen referred through the Boston Private Industry Council. The approximate weekly salary is $235 and the duration of the program is six to eight weeks.

Employment: Send a cover letter and résumé to the Human Resources Department when applying for a full-time job. Approximately fifty to seventy-five entry-level people are hired each year. Preferably, candidates should apply for specific job assignments. The approximate salary range for entry-level people in editorial jobs is $22,000 to $24,000. A personal interview is required. In addition to job-specific skills, everyone must have outstanding communications skills both written and oral; commitment to excellence; intellectual curiosity; and a strong work ethic. Twenty to 30 percent of new hires are employed in editorial assignments.

Little, Brown and Company
34 Beacon Street
Boston, MA 02118
(617) 227-0730
Contact: Steven Lee

Internships: The company offers a summer internship program from June through August at a salary of $250 a week. Closing date for applications is April 1. Send résumé and cover letter. Interns are hired between junior and senior college years, and about 10 percent of interns are hired for full-time jobs. Company evaluates performance of interns.

Employment: Send cover letter and résumé when applying for a full-time job. Approximately forty entry-level people are hired each year, and candidates should apply for specific job assignments. Starting salary for entry-level people in editorial jobs is $20,000 to $21,000. A personal interview is required and about 20 percent of new hires are employed in editorial assignments.

Training: The company conducts an organized training program for new employees that lasts for three months. There is a formal training program evaluation.

W. W. Norton & Company
500 Fifth Avenue
New York, NY 10110
(212) 354-5500

This company does not offer an internship program.

Employment: Approximately five entry-level people are hired each year. Candidates should apply for specific job assignments. The approximate salary range for entry-level people in editorial jobs is $18,000 to $20,000. A personal interview is required. Prospective employees must possess a good general education and interest in books. Sixty percent of new hires are employed in editorial assignments.

The Reader's Digest Association
261 Madison Avenue
New York, NY 10016
(212) 850-7000
Contact: Human Resources Department

Internships: The company offers a summer internship program for eight to twelve weeks at a salary of $375 a week for undergrads. College major preferences are journalism, English, marketing, finance, and liberal arts. Closing date for applications is March 1. Applicants should send a cover letter with dates of availability and areas of interest, such as ad sales, circulation, promotion, and editorial. Interns are hired between junior and senior college years and about 50 percent are hired for full-time jobs. Interns rotate between departments and their performance is evaluated.

Employment: To apply, send résumé and cover letter. About ten entry-level people are hired each year at a salary of $20,000 to $25,000 for editorial jobs. Candidates should apply for specific job assignments and a personal interview is required. Prospective employees must possess such basic skills as excellent oral/written communication skills; organizational skills; PC proficiency with word processing and spreadsheets. About 20 percent of new hires are employed in editorial assignments.

St. Martin's Press
175 Fifth Avenue
New York, NY 10010
(212) 674-5151
Contact: Helaine Ohl, Personnel Manager

Internships: This company does not have a formal internship program. Employees are hired for summer jobs depending on staffing needs at an hourly rate of $7 per hour.

Employment: Applicants should send their résumé with cover letter to the Personnel Department. Yearly hiring policy for entry-level people varies. Seventy-five entry-level people were hired in 1993 due to company expansion. Candidates may apply for a specific job, but it is not required. The approximate salary range for entry-level people in editorial jobs is high teens. A personal interview is required. Employees should possess excellent organization, communication, computer, and typing skills.

John Wiley & Sons
605 Third Avenue
New York, NY 10158
(212) 850-6000
Contact: Human Resources Department

Internships: The company offers a summer internship program for approximately nine weeks at a salary of $300 a week. Closing date of applications is April 1. Send résumé and cover letter specifying areas of interest. A liberal arts major is preferred. Interns are hired between junior and senior college years and about 40 percent are hired for full-time jobs. Interns sometimes rotate between departments and participating managers assess performance by completing questionnaires at the end of the program.

Employment: Send résumé and cover letter when applying for a full-time job expressing interest in and benefits to be gained from employment in company. Approximately seventy entry-level people are hired each year. Candidates should apply for specific job assignments and a personal interview is required. Prospective employees should possess basic skills in computers (word processing, spreadsheets), basic office skills, and the ability to prioritize and organize a heavy work load. About 30 to 40 percent of new hires are employed in editorial assignments.

Training: The company has an organized training program for new employees. Duration of the program varies, and there is a formal training program evaluation. In addition to a New Employee Orientation Program (one-half day), the company offers training programs (duration varies) in three curriculum areas: self-management skills, leadership/management skills, and business/technical publishing.

Names and Addresses of Other Large Publishers

Bantam Doubleday Dell
Publishing Group
1540 Broadway
New York, NY 10036
(212) 354-6500

Grolier
Sherman Turnpike
Danbury, CT 06816
(203) 797-3500

Harcourt Brace Jovanovich
525 B Street, Suite 1900
San Diego, CA 93101
(619) 699-6707

HarperCollins Publishers
10 East 53rd Street
New York, NY 10003
(212) 207-7000

Henry Holt & Co
115 West 15th Street
New York, NY 10011
(212) 886-9200

Macmillan Publishing USA
201 West 103rd Street
Indianapolis, IN 46290
(317) 581-3500

McGraw-Hill
1221 Avenue of the Americas
New York, NY 10020
(212) 512-2000

Oxford University Press
200 Madison Avenue
New York, NY 10016
(212) 679-7300

Penguin USA
375 Hudson Street
New York, NY 10014
(212) 366-2000

Prentice Hall
One Lake Street
Upper Saddle River, NJ 07428
(201) 236-7000

The Putnam Publishing Group
200 Madison Avenue
New York, NY 10016
(212) 951-8400

Time Life Books
777 Duke Street
Alexandria, VA 22314
(703) 838-7000

Random House
201 East 50th Street
New York, NY 10022
(212) 751-2600

Warner Books
1271 Avenue of the Americas
New York, NY 10020
(212) 522-5279

Simon & Schuster Trade Group
1230 Avenue of the Americas
New York, NY 10020
(212) 698-7000

Western Publishing
1220 Mound Avenue
Racine, WI 53404
(414) 633-2431

Book publishing is a creative profession and you must adapt a creative strategy to break in. In addition to the specific suggestions outlined in this chapter, candidates should gain some experience in standard office skills and in the tools of modern technology such as computers, video terminals, and even desktop publishing. In applying, you should also make preliminary decisions on which area of publishing you would like to enter.

Glossary of Publishing Terms

◆

ABA. The American Booksellers Association; within the trade, the abbreviation often refers to the association's annual convention.

adoption. The selection and approval of a book for school or college use.

advance. The sum paid to an author by a publisher before a book's publication recouped by the publisher from the book's sales.

auction. Bidding for a book's rights by various publishers.

backlist. List of books published in a previous season and still available for sale; titles selling steadily year after year.

binding. The manufacturing process that folds, gathers, and stitches or glues body pages to a cover.

book club. Publisher that issues special editions that are marketed to the club's members.

case binding. The dominant binding system for hardcover books.

copyediting. The review of a manuscript before typesetting for grammar, spelling, punctuation, and style.

copyright. The legal right granted to a literary work.

desktop publishing. The computer-aided factor used in a book's production to quickly and efficiently process, tailor, or revise graphics and typesetting.

elhi. A designation for textbooks for use in elementary and high schools (kindergarten through twelfth grade).

first serial rights. The sale of a portion of a book to a magazine, newspaper, or periodical before a book's publication.

Frankfurt Book Fair. An international convocation held in Frankfurt, Germany, primarily for the exchange of book rights.

galleys. Paper or photocopy proofs of a book's text pulled before platemaking and printing.

imprint. The name of a book's publisher printed on the title page or elsewhere, usually with the place and date of publication.

juvenile. A category of books for children.

literary agent. An author's representative in his or her relationship with a publisher.

LMP. *Literary Market Place,* an important industry directory.

mass market. The book market, most often for paperbacks sold to bookstores and mass outlets such as drugstores, department stores, and supermarkets.

packager. An individual or company who performs editorial and production services for a book that is marketed and distributed by a publisher.

remainders. Copies of books remaining in the publisher's stock when its sale has practically ceased, frequently sold at a reduced price.

returns. Books not sold by a bookseller and returned to the publisher.

royalties. An agreed portion of the income from a book paid to its author, usually a percentage of the retail price of each copy sold.

special sales. Sales made other than to bookstores.

subsidiary rights. An important source of additional revenue for a publisher, whereby the rights to a book are sold for book club distribution, paperback reprint, magazine serialization, translation into foreign editions, and motion picture adaptation.

textbook. A book used by students as a standard work for a particular branch of study; often contains special exercises and tests.

trade book. A book designed for the general public and available through an ordinary book dealer, as distinguished from a limited-edition book, a textbook, or a mass-market paperback.

trade paperback. A softbound book sold in bookstores, often larger than a mass-market paperback.

Recommended Reading

$\blacklozenge$

Appelbaum, Judith. *How to Get Happily Published.* New York: HarperCollins, 1992.

Bailey, Herbert S., Jr. *The Art and Science of Book Publishing.* Athens, OH: Ohio University Press, 1990.

R. R. Bowker Co. *Getting Into Book Publishing.* 2nd ed. New York: R. R. Bowker Co., 1983. (Pamphlet: Single copy free.)

Collier, Oscar, with Frances Spatz Leighton. *How to Write and Sell Your First Nonfiction Book.* New York: St. Martin's Press, 1990.

Curtis, Richard. *Beyond the Bestseller: A Literary Agent Takes You Inside the Book Business.* New York: Plume, 1990.

Delton, Judy. *The 29 Most Common Writing Mistakes and How to Avoid Them.* Cincinnati: Writer's Digest Books, 1991.

Dessauer, John P. *Book Publishing: A Basic Introduction.* New York: Continuum, 1993.

Emerson, Connie. *The Writer's Guide to Conquering the Magazine Market.* Cincinnati: Writer's Digest Books, 1991.

Fulton, Len, ed. *International Directory of Little Magazines and Small Presses.* Paradise, CA: Dustbooks, 1992.

Geiser, Elizabeth, and Arnold Dolin, eds. *The Business of Book Publishing.* Boulder, CO: Westview Press, 1985.

Herman, Jeff. *Insider's Guide to Book Editors, Publishers, and Literary Agents: Who They Are! What They Want! and How to Win Them Over!* Rocklin, CA: Prima Publishing, 1994/95 ed.

Koller, Edward. *The Hiring Challenge.* Stamford, CT: Cowles Business Media, 1991.

Potter, Clarkson N. *Who Does What and Why in Book Publishing: Writers, Editors and Money Men.* New York: Carol Publishing Group, 1990.

Rogers, Geoffrey. *Editing for Print.* Cincinnati: Writer's Digest Books, 1985.

Ross, Tom, and Marilyn Ross. *The Complete Guide to Self-Publishing.* Cincinnati: Writer's Digest Books, 1990.

University of Chicago Press. *The Chicago Manual of Style.* 14th ed. Chicago: University of Chicago Press, 1993.

Writer's Digest Books. *1994 Writer's Market: Where and How to Sell What You Write.* Cincinnati: Writer's Digest Books, 1994.

Index